The Career Management Challenge

The Career Management Challenge
Balancing Individual and Organizational Needs

Peter Herriot

SAGE Publications
London • Thousand Oaks • New Delhi

First published 1992, Reprinted 1994

 SAGE Publications Ltd
6 Bonhill Street
London EC2A 4PU

SAGE Publications Inc
2455 Teller Road
Thousand Oaks, California 91320

SAGE Publications India Pvt Ltd
32, M-Block Market
Greater Kailash - 1
New Delhi 110 048

British Library Cataloguing in Publication Data

A catalogue record for this book is available from the
British Library.

ISBN 0 8039 8655 6
ISBN 0 8039 8656 4 (pbk)

Library of Congress catalog card number 92–050202

Typeset by Mayhew Typesetting, Rhayader, Powys
Printed in Great Britain by J. W. Arrowsmith Ltd, Bristol

Contents

Acknowledgements

I would like to thank the following colleagues for their help with this book: Gill Adamson, Malcolm Ballantine, Gavin Barrett, Lyn Black, John Blakey, Rupert Eales-White, Philip Foster, Sue Jones, Anne Kellitt, Jenny Kidd, Ron Lord, Carole Pemberton, Rob Pinder, Rosemary Rowntree, Nick Rushby, Eric Schlesinger and Bryan Smith.

1
Why Careers?

Who owns your career? The use of the possessive pronoun implies that *you* do. In which case, how is it that organisations keep referring to *their* career management systems and to *their* human resources? The central argument of this book is that there cannot be a winner in this tug-of-war. Only those organisations which negotiate careers will keep the people they need to help them survive the next decade.

For the changes of the next decade, many of which are already upon us, threaten the very existence of many organisations. The degree of turmoil they are experiencing leads us to doubt whether they, or we, can cope. Charles Handy's *The Future of Work* and *The Age of Unreason* have brilliantly alerted us.[1] But what can we do about it? One thing that's quite clear is that the answer will involve people. The old cliché 'an organisation's most valuable asset is its people' doesn't go far enough. An organisation *is* its people.

Nevertheless, 'career' sounds a pretty odd candidate for the 'big idea' of the 90s. At first sight, it wouldn't win many general elections among human resource (HR) professionals, let alone among hard-nosed managers. One thing the 80s have shown us, they would say, is that the old idea of cradle to grave, man and boy is dead. Careers for life can't even be left to the few giants like IBM and Shell who used to be able to afford them. Things have long ago moved on for the rest of us. And now we're in the depth of recession, talking of careers is a sick joke.

Career metaphors

But who talked about careers for life? There is a whole set of career metaphors which actively conceal the essence of the idea of career. Life in the organisational womb is just one of them. Others are plentiful and equally misleading; for example, careers as 'climbing the ladder', implying that the only worthwhile career move is upwards. We hear of careers as 'game plans', a lifelong chess match in which sacrificing your bishop now has implications for three moves ahead. Or there's careers as 'paths', sequences of jobs well trodden before by eminent others, which lead to some-where desirable in the end; if you are lucky, your organisation will map these out for you. Perhaps most grandiloquent of all is careers as 'pyramids', carefully and painfully constructed edifices of achievement, with the major building blocks supporting the crown-ing glory.

Of course, there are less exalted metaphors, more favoured by the cynical. Careers are a 'rat race', with the survival of the nastiest as the Darwinian principle. Or they are 'court intrigue' with stabs in the back to be constantly guarded against. Every other business play on the television reinforces this one. Bringing warfare more up to date, careers are a 'minefield' – you have to be really careful each step you take, otherwise you're blown up or, at the least, diverted off course.

The less cynical and the less grandiloquent among us may harbour a couple of more modest metaphors: career as 'timetable', and career as 'tournament'. If we haven't attained a certain level by a certain age, then, we feel, we've blown our chances. We're behind timetable, and it's going to be impossible to catch up. And why have we fallen behind? Because we've done badly in one of the rounds of the tournament – we didn't get promoted to middle management first time round.

Given these metaphors for careers, it's hardly surprising that the idea of career doesn't seem at first sight to be a good candidate for the big idea of the 90s. After all, many of these metaphors imply that things will continue much as they have in the past. Ladders and pyramids imply multi-level organisational structures which we now see being rapidly stripped down. Paths, timetables, and chess matches imply a level of predictability which we know doesn't exist any longer. Tournaments, rat races and court intrigues are peopled by individuals whose one aim in life is to get promoted; but we sense that quality of life concerns a lot of people these days more than does promotion.

Careers in time

So at first blush, the speed of change seems to render career an outmoded idea. Nothing could be further from the truth. The idea of career is central to the 90s for the very reason that it is the only idea which *can* cope with the changes that assail us at the end of the twentieth century. This is, as Michael Arthur and others remind us,[2] because it tackles head-on the three major HR issues of our time.

First, the career idea is about *time*. It looks at the present in the light both of the past, as the individual and the organisation have experienced it, and also of the projected future. Because it has this dynamic quality, it makes sense of change. It enables us to understand why we are where we are now in the light of where we've been before; but it also points up the magnitude of the jump to where we might have to get. Ten years ago the big retail banks could look back on solid achievements. Their career structures were firmly in place; employees had clear ideas of where they might go, how they might get there, and the training and development that were required. The job tasks were known and defined, and the future looked as though it would continue to be fairly like the past. Then the prospect of deregulation loomed on the horizon. The notion that jobs and the skills required for them would remain the same as in the past had to be jettisoned.

Organisational structures and sequences of career positions were grist to the competitive mill, for now the banks had no monopoly in any of their services and needed to challenge other providers in their markets too. The human resource implications for the financial sector are only just being thought through; hence the deserved popularity of such reports as Amin Rajan's on manpower in the City of London.[3]

So in an era of change, an excessive faith that the past is a good guide to the future on the part of individual and organisation has the Fool's Paradise consequence shown in Figure 1.1; this figure relates the extent to which individuals and organisations are focused on the past or the future and on what happens when these perspectives coincide or differ. Of course, individuals may trust their own past experience as a guide to the future when their organisation has moved on in its thinking – 'hard cheese', alas, for people who have failed to read the signs in the outside world. Smart alecs have done just that, but haven't convinced their organisations – or more likely, haven't tried to. Individuals and organisations who perceive change and as a consequence construe their futures differently from their pasts are ready for 'onward careers'.

Careers in organisations

This brings us on to the next feature of the career concept which makes it the big idea for the 90s. Organisational careers are *relationships over time between individuals and their organisations*. This seems so obvious as not to be worth saying, but there are strong forces operating against it at this very moment. There is a possibility that the current emphasis on HR strategy may highlight

	Organisation Past	Organisation Future
Individual Past	Fool's Paradise	Hard Cheese
Individual Future	Smart Alec	Onward Career

Figure 1.1   *Past versus future career emphasis*

the organisation's use of its human resources at the expense of individuals' own needs and preferences. Indeed, the very use of the phrase 'human resources' carries a hint of this danger. Introduced for the very good reason that people are of more value than money, it also has the connotation of ownership. Organisations must 'use' the human resources that they 'own' wisely, and 'develop' them so that they get the most 'benefit' out of them. Most recent HR textbooks have this strong managerialist flavour.[4] On the other hand, nurturing, husbanding and investing in people is a big improvement on the dry administrative odour of 'personnel'.

You can see why the human resource terminology has become popular. Organisations have to maintain themselves in existence, and do so by adapting fast. They can achieve these fundamental aims only if their people are organised so as to achieve current business objectives. This means ensuring that people with the right skills are doing the right thing at the right time. Managing the careers of individuals so that they are ready to fill the new jobs which business needs imply is a major concern. Gone are the old days when succession planning meant listing a couple of people a year before the present job incumbent is due to retire. Instead, organisations have to develop their people so that they are flexible enough to meet new challenges and fill new jobs. By way of example, Royal Mail (Letters) introduced a total quality programme recently. As a consequence over fifty quality control managers most of them from within, were appointed one to each of the district offices – every one of them a newly created job designed to achieve a new corporate business objective.

So organisations have come to realise that they need to 'develop and use their human resources' effectively. But the individual is in another ball park. The individual's career is frequently considered their own business – the organisation only intervenes at the individual level when it feels it has a moral duty to do so: individual career counselling is often provided only when people are made redundant or about to retire. In her recent well-received 'When Giants Learn to Dance', Rosabeth Moss Kanter[5] notes this dissociation between the organisation and the individual. Today's and tomorrow's knowledge workers have one main career concern, she argues: they want to increase their marketability in the labour market. They do so by adding to their knowledge and skills and keeping them right up to date. They can be periodically caught gleefully stealing off to the disc containing their CV to add another line or two. Their careers are professional ones between organisations, not managerial ones within them. Kanter offers little advice or prediction about how such individuals' aspirations and organisational HR needs can be reconciled.

But there are lots of other employees besides professionals. And the idea of an organisational career is as important to them as it is to their organisations. Many people are expected to surrender a great deal for their organisations; they need to know what they are likely to get back. How can the two parties' sets of expectations be reconciled? Two sets of questions will be asked at the end of each chapter: what do careers mean for the individual reader? And what do they mean for his or her organisation?

So there are key unsolved issues here. Organisations want to make use of people, but they are often unaware of what those people want for themselves. They expect commitment and performance, and think they can engineer it by performance-related pay and other material inducements. What they don't always realise is that it is individuals with whom they are dealing. Individuals differ in their aspirations; these change during the course of their lives, and there are great social movements afoot which will affect what is generally valued and what is not. Since the idea of career implies a two-way relationship between individual and organisation, it meets an immediate need in the 90s, for we are currently obsessed with a one-way top-down management perspective.

Careers in the head

The third and last feature of the career concept is the distinction between internal and external, or *subjective and objective* careers. Yes, you can plot the positions that a person has held, the functional units they have served in, the levels they have reached, and how long they spent in each job. Some very interesting things can come out of this. In the 70s in the USA, for example, one of the best predictors of how far up an organisation a person went was how long they spent in their first job in it.[6] At the aggregate organisational level, you can look at career paths and see the number of employees at each level, whether they were promoted from below or came from outside, and so on.[7]

But the *subjective* perceptions of organisational careers are equally important. Am I on track, behind time, or ahead of schedule in the career timetable?[8] Were there some crucial rounds of the tournament I missed out on?[9] How fairly have I been treated relative to the others who started with me? What is it that helps people get on round here – visibility? patronage? effectiveness? experience? And what about the organisational career culture? Manpower flows and the extent of internal promotion are merely objective surface manifestations. What are the underlying organisational values and assumptions about careers?

Perhaps it is widely assumed in the organisation that

- people only work for the financial rewards;
- people are appointed to fill particular jobs;
- everyone wants promotion;
- you're past it at 50.

The concept of career has both an objective, external side, and a subjective, internal one. It recognises that beliefs and values, expectations and aspirations, are just as important as sequences of positions held and aggregate manpower flows. What's more, the subjective approach isn't going to separate one's organisational career from the rest of one's life in the same neat and tidy way as an objective account.

So instead of looking for keys to successful careers, we've settled on careers as the key to success. Career-thinking helps us come to terms with rapid change over time; it brings together the individual's and the organisation's expectations in a coincidence of interests; and it relates historical events to subjective experience.

The psychological contract

Psychological contracting between individual and organisation is the process which holds the whole organisational enterprise together. It is the invisible glue which binds individuals to the organisation over time. It incorporates the parties' beliefs, values, expectations and aspirations. The individual's objective, external career is the sequence of the positions he or she holds in the organisation, but their subjective internal career is the process of psychological contracting.

The famous American organisational psychologist, Chris Argyris,[10] was originally responsible for the concept of the psychological contract. He implied that a psychological contract was always operating over and above the formal contract of employment. He defined it as a set of *mutually agreed expectations* between the two parties. So, for example, ten years ago people employed by UK retail banks and insurance companies held an expectation of a job for life, and their organisations encouraged them in this by tying them in with various benefits, for example low mortgages. The organisation, on the other hand, expected loyalty in exchange for this security, and a move to a competitor was construed as treachery.

This example points to another feature of the psychological contract – *it isn't necessarily made explicit.* Indeed, for many organisations it was part of the implicit culture which people picked up by osmosis and observation. When a young bank clerk saw an obviously incompetent assistant manager of 50 shunted into a non-job until retirement, she soon cottoned on. One of the basic assumptions of the bank culture was that people never lost their jobs except for misdemeanour; and one of the key values was a concern for employees' well-being at the cost of a loss of efficiency.

Explicit contracting, on the other hand, is usually a prescription of what ought to happen rather than a description of what actually goes on. Our 50-year-old assistant manager should probably have engaged in career discussions with his or her boss over time. The bank could then have discovered what the employee really wanted, and the employee might have realised that a major change in career was inevitable. The outcome might then have been an agreement more satisfactory to both parties – part-time employment, perhaps.

Another feature of the psychological contract which makes it ideal as 'career glue' is its *continual renegotiation.* Psychological contracts aren't set in tablets of stone – they change. At any one point in time we can take a snapshot of the contract, but that's merely a fix on a moving target. Organisations' expectations change and so do individuals' – which is why a contract that meets some of both today may meet few of either in a year or two's time. The bank might realise that a demographic decrease in the number of school leavers means that greater resources need to be put into school liaison; the assistant manager arrives at a point in his career when he realises he doesn't want promotion to manager and he'd like more contact with young people. Neither of these expectations were held a couple of years before; both parties' expectations and interests have fortuitously coincided at a given moment. Unfortunately, the organisation's current needs and those of individuals aren't always so conveniently in synch; and anyway, in our example, there was no communication.

A really sensitive boss would have picked up the assistant manager's change of heart; a well-informed assistant manager would have seen the demographic opportunity, and an implicit agreement could possibly have been reached. A regular career meeting could have made expectations and psychological contract explicit: from now on the assistant manager was off the promotion ladder. It's worth noting in parenthesis that the failure to negotiate a psychological contract doesn't necessarily imply the end of the employment contract. People and organisations can soldier unhappily on expecting different things of each other and feeling cheated when they don't happen. The archetypal plateaued manager still harbours promotion ambitions while the organisation wants him or her to be motivated enough to learn new tricks at their present level.

So the ideas of change, career and contract have given us a process framework for looking at people in organisations in the 90s. Figure 1.2 puts it graphically. First of all we have the overall framework of time, moving from left to right. At the core of the process are the individual and the organisation. The psychological contract between them is represented by the central line with dots, implying repeated renegotiations. Exit points from the contract are indicated by the arrows, which may sometimes imply severance of the employment contract itself. After all, the length of time individuals spend in one organisation varies hugely. The outer lines represent the environment in which organisation and individual exist, and which affect both continuously. The changing political, economic and business environment produces changes in organisations' strategy, structure and culture. The changing social environment leads individuals to have new aspirations and expectations about their work. In terms of Figure 1.2, then, we can arrive at a new definition of career: *An organisational career is the sequence of renegotiations of the psychological contract which the individual and the organisation conduct during his or her period of employment.*

The career idea having been introduced in this chapter, it is the framework of Figure 1.2 which determines the structure of the rest of this book. We'll look at the business environment of the 90s with its sea changes, many of them already upon us, in chapter 2.

Chapter 3 will consider what sort of expectations organisations will hold of their employees. What sort of people will they want, and how will they expect them to develop?

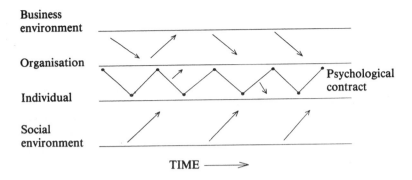

Figure 1.2 *Careering through the 90s*

In chapter 4 we move down to the bottom of the figure, and ask what are the great social movements of our time, those changes of heart and mind which clever politicians sniff in the wind? For it is these which affect individuals' expectations, these which form the frame for the wide range of individual differences. Quality of life matters – for some it will mean that family come first, for others refusal to work for an environmentally hostile employer. Employees' expectations are also outlined in chapter 4.

But the overall point of Figure 1.2 is crystal clear. The career concept provides a way of looking at the changing psychological contract in its changing environment. There's no point in looking at change just from the organisation's point of view, from the top down: that results in ever-increasing and unsupportable demands on the individual. There's equally little point in idealistic notions of individual fulfilment outside organisational frameworks. Most work involves co-operating in organisations, so for most of us a psychological contract has to be struck and restruck. Chapter 5 is devoted to the values necessary if balances are to be struck between organisational and individual expectations, and to the apparently parlous state of the psychological contract in the UK at present. Chapter 6 seeks to explain this unhappy situation in terms of the strategic changes now sweeping through organisations. Culture change programmes and the human resources movement are seen as only partial responses. The remainder of the book looks at how each of these contractual balances will be achieved by the organisational survivors of the 90s. Four balances are explored: those between the organisation's need for change and the individual's expectation of support (chapter 7); between loyalty and respect (chapter 8); between knowledge and tolerance (chapter 9); and between intelligence and trust (chapter 10). Chapter 11 gets back to individuals, and suggests some career balances they may achieve.

Culture change

But why choose these particular Cs – career and contract? Organisations are constantly seeking to catch up strategically with the huge and rapid changes in their business environment. Why not a few strategic ideas which are current favourites? In response to the biggest C of all, change, a small army of other Cs have achieved prominence, and their own fierce devotees. It is only when we see the shortcomings of each of these that career and contract become stronger runners. The first is imposed culture change.

Ed Schein wrote the classic analysis of *organisational culture*.[11] He claimed it took him years even to understand an organisation's culture. For Schein, culture was expressed in *artifacts*, the outward and visible signs of underlying realities: a company's office, its appraisal form, the titles it gives its managers, the myths and stories which go the rounds. Their main use is as one source of evidence about these deeper realities – values and assumptions. *Values* are quite often expressed – 'It's the bottom line that's important round here.' *Assumptions* are usually implicit and taken for granted. The analyst might tease out such beliefs as 'People work for the money', or 'Everyone wants promotion.' Culture serves to hold the organisation together – a common culture like a national culture. But just as we sometimes overestimate the degree of national identity, so we may ignore subcultural differences between businesses or functions within a corporate organisation. Culture is also supposed to help organisations adapt, by changing in accord with external environmental changes. The job-for-life values of some financial institutions are changing in response to the opening up of market competition. Understanding the cultures of organisations is crucial to careering through the 90s; but explicit attempts to change organisational culture by diktat from on high are entirely another matter.

A 'cultural engineering' solution to change has recently become fashionable. This aims both to create a unified organisational culture and to change existing culture(s) to match changed business environments. Artifacts have often been the first target – new names, new logos, new systems. But values and, above all, assumptions have proved more stubborn. For example, chief executives have been prevailed upon to reward people who make mistakes in an effort to encourage sensible risk taking. But isolated signals such as these seldom percolate through to the middle management layers where they matter.

Customer care and client-first programmes are types of culture change programme. Recent examples have stressed that internal clients and customers are just as important as external ones. This is in response to the resentment of employees who are asked to treat customers better than they are treated themselves. Underlying the difficulties of nearly all culture change programmes is one single shortcoming: the programme is imposed from above. The purpose may have been absolutely appropriate – many organisations need to be more responsive to their customers or clients. But the method is frequently wrong; most culture change programmes ignore the need to contract. Engineered culture change lacks the reciprocity of the idea of career; and it is a mass, not an individualised intervention.

Commitment

In their efforts to cope with change, organisations have stressed another recent big C: commitment. Employees are urged to be committed to their organisation and to their work. Peters and Waterman in *In Search of Excellence*[12] give example after example of individuals making great personal sacrifices in order to achieve what their organisation expected of them. But a *reciprocal* commitment to the individual isn't so common. Again, the relationship is often a one-sided one; the organisation usually holds the cards and calls the tune. Whether the relationship can be so one-sided in the future is another matter – in a seller's labour market it is the employee who holds the power advantage, but in the present recession, the organisation doesn't need to negotiate a psychological contract with most of its employees if it doesn't want to. Only when organisations believe that employees have rights will psychological contracting carry on, whatever the economic climate.

Competencies

The final rival C is the idea of individual competencies – or rather the ideas, since there's not much clarity about what's meant by the term. Competencies are generally considered to be people's capacities in the various areas of functioning considered part of their work. Strategic planning or oral communication are examples. Following the Management Charter Initiative,[13] different competencies are assumed to be necessary for different levels of managerial work. The assumption is, however, that competencies are equally appropriate to different jobs at a particular level, and to work in different organisations.

In the modern HR climate, competencies sound an ideal tool. They enable the organisation to monitor individuals' development in various areas and allocate them to groups available to fill positions at a certain level. They also provide individuals with guidelines for self-development, so that they can acquire or refine competencies in order to develop themselves and meet the organisation's business requirements.

There's one thing about the idea of competencies which is a bit limiting, though. It has a rather static feel about it. Are we sure that work will remain the same in the future, requiring the same competencies at the same levels? If there's one thing the last decade has taught us, it is that a high proportion of the jobs to which people move are newly created ones. And the higher the level of the job, the more likely the new incumbent is to adapt it to himself or herself. In their comprehensive review of managerial job change in the UK, Nigel Nicholson and Michael West found that more than half of the jobs to which managers moved were new ones.[14] Clearly some of the currently quoted competencies will always be needed, especially interpersonal and team skills. But, overall, the major competency will be that of acquiring new competencies.

So culture change and commitment miss out the individual's point of view, while the competencies movement isn't dynamic enough over time. The career idea includes both parties in the psychological contract, and it permits past and future perspectives to illuminate the present.

Perhaps most important of all, the psychological contract is at the core of the career concept, as Figure 1.2 demonstrates. The implication is that if there is no contract, organisations' attempts to adapt to change are likely to run into difficulties. It is the nature of the contract which determines the direction of change as much as the converse; people whose prime career expectation is to be able to meet patients' health care needs are not going to permit a cultural change which makes cost efficiency a prior value, as the UK National Health Service is finding out fast. On the other hand, as we shall see, part of the individual's contract may be to develop their knowledge and skills so as to be able to cope with change.

Some final questions

About your own career

- How would you complete the sentence: My career is like a ___?
- How would you complete the sentence: My career will be like a ___?
- In which quadrant of Figure 1.1 do you fit?
- Do you have a career timetable? Are you ahead, on time, or behind it?
- If yes, how did you get to know what it is?
- What are the three or four most important expectations that you hold of the organisation? And the same for the organisation's expectations of you?
- How satisfied are you with this psychological contract?

About your organisation

- What are the current assumptions in your organisation about careers within it?
- What are the policy statements made about careers?
- How do the two differ? Why do they differ?
- How has your organisation's approach to careers changed over the past few years?

Notes

1 C. Handy, (1985) *The Future of Work.* Oxford: Basil Blackwell; C. Handy, (1989) *The Age of Unreason.* London: Business Books.

2 M.B. Arthur, D.T. Hall B.S. Lawrence (1989) *Handbook of Career Theory.* Cambridge: Cambridge University Press.

3 A. Rajan (1988) 'Today the City, tomorrow . . . managing a knowledge economy', *Personnel Management*, October: 30–7.

4 C. Fombrun, N.M. Tichy and M.A. Devanna (eds) (1984) *Strategic Human Resource Management.* New York: John Wiley; W.J. Rothwell and H.C. Kazanas (1989) *Strategic Human Resource Development.* Englewood Cliffs, NJ: Prentice-Hall; L. Nadler and G.D. Wiggs (1988) *Managing Human Resource Development.* San Francisco: Jossey-Bass.

5 R.M. Kanter (1989) *When Giants Learn to Dance.* New York: Simon & Schuster.

6 J.F. Veiga (1983) 'Mobility influences during managerial career stages', *Academy of Management Journal*, 26: 64–85.

7 M. Bennison and J.Casson (1984) *The Manpower Planning Handbook.* London: McGraw-Hill.

8 B. Lawrence (1984) 'Age-grading: the implicit organisational timetable', *Journal of Occupational Behaviour*, 5: 23–35.

9 J.E. Rosenbaum (1979) 'Tournament mobility: career patterns in a corporation', *Administrative Science Quarterly*, 24: 220–41.

10 C. Argyris (1960) *Understanding Organisational Behaviour*. Homewood, Illinois: Dorsey Press.

11 E.H. Schein (1985) *Organisational Culture and Leadership*. San Francisco: Jossey-Bass.

12 T.J. Peters and R.H. Waterman (1981) *In Search of Excellence*. New York: Harper & Row.

13 M. Day (1988) 'Managerial competence and the charter initiative', *Personnel Management*, August: 30–4; V. Dulewicz (1989) 'Assessment centres as the route to competence', *Personnel Management*, November: 56–9.

14 N. Nicholson and M. West (1989) *Managerial Job Change: Men and Women in Transition*. Cambridge: Cambridge University Press.

2
Business Trends

Crystal balls

Crystal ball gazers vary from the vaguely sublime to the specifically ridiculous. From the vague end come such portentous clichés as 'The only thing we can predict about the future is its unpredictability.' From the specific end we have confident certainties like 'By the year 1995 there will be 5 million teleworkers in Britain.'

There must surely be a happy medium or, rather, a happy crystal ball gazer. We need to look at the consequences for organisations of current trends which we can be reasonably confident will continue. This way we'll avoid the pitfalls of specific prophecies about the implications of technological change. We won't fall into such traps as predicting the total replacement of documents by the ubiquitous VDU. We'll also refuse the hopeless task of predicting the nature of the next major technological revolution.

And when we consider the political and economic environment we'll be even more cautious; the general momentum towards European unity may be unstoppable, but who could have predicted the rapidity of the dismantling of the Soviet empire? Even events of which we can be absolutely confident – the demographic dip in school-leavers in the present decade for example – may not have direct and obvious implications for organisations.

We'll focus on such general trends as:

- the sea changes in technology which have already happened;
- recent transformations in the universal consciousness, such as concern about the environment;
- the labour market, the context in which both the employment and the psychological contracts are made.

In this chapter we are concerned with the implications of these environmental trends for organisations. For as they realise what is hitting them, organisations will have ever more demanding expectations of their employees. Thus the business environment is crucial to the nature of careers and the psychological contract. For it will determine one side of the contract: what organisations expect of their employees.

As we look at the last few decades, a sequence of general business trends can be detected. These trends are spearheaded by the world leaders in their markets – the Canons, Xeroxes and Hondas. They have anticipated environmental change, or at the very least reacted to it with speed and vigour. When others were acquiring new businesses with gay abandon which were unrelated to their core competencies, they were divesting. When others were decentralising and delegating corporate responsibilities to strategic business units, they were retaining at the centre much more than just overall financial control. And now that others are subcontracting essential parts of their research, design, production or marketing functions, they are busily acquiring by means of strategic alliances any knowledge in these core areas which they lack themselves.

So if we want to see how organisations in general will be responding to environmental trends, one thing we can do is to look at how the world leaders are already responding. But we need to be careful here as well; what is true of leading-edge global winners in hi-tech manufacturing industry is unlikely to be true now or in the near future for many nationally based organisations. It's also totally alien to East European organisations, whose first step will have to be away from stifling centralised bureaucracy. Nevertheless, what the global leaders are doing now is likely to be immediately relevant for any organisation aiming to become an international player. And it is likely to be relevant in the longer run even for those aiming at a limited nationally based segment of the market.

So we've made crystal-ball gazing a bit more respectable; we can feel more comfortable looking at existing trends rather than gazing ahead with wild surmise. But we can't feel at all comfortable when we look at what those trends are and what implications they have for organisations. In particular, there is grave concern about what will be expected of individuals and how they will manage their careers.

The technological tornado

Technological change is transforming organisations, as Kim Clark among many others, has stressed.[1] A variety of technologically based capacities are acting together, driving profound adaptations both inside the organisation and at its interface with its environment. Each individual technological application is a wind of change; taken together they're a tornado. How is it that their total effect is greater than their individual sum?

Let's start first with *the invention and design* of the goods or services which are the organisation's *raison d'être*. Everyone's familiar with the idea of a technological advance, such as the microchip, making possible a new type of product, such as the personal computer. What we often fail to realise is that typically, advanced products or services depend upon several leading-edge technologies, not just one. The laser printer is an example of this synergy. And the creativity in designing new products and services doesn't just mean spotting new uses for single technologies; it means combining technologies in new ways.

Technological control of production and of service provision is a second powerful wind of organisational change. Process control technology is now flexible enough to provide a wide range of varieties on a theme. Improved communications have made the world aware of the existence of theme products or services. Process control technology can build individuality into them. It can satisfy different styles and tastes, the expressions of different national and regional cultures. And it can meet people's increasing need to own a product or receive a service different from that which others have. Instead of the cultural imperialism of a McDonald's hamburger in Moscow, or a Benetton sweater in Birmingham, it's possible to have national varieties of the same global product. You can see the results of such customisation in the worldwide variety of televisions sold by the same manufacturer and using the same range of components.

The third IT wind of change is the *amount of information* which can be aggregated and transmitted immediately. Senior managers of a retail corporation can have summary figures of today's overall sales and profits. Middle managers can scan today's regional sales of a particular product in their supermarket chain and adjust prices and replenish stocks accordingly. Research and development project leaders can leave administrative detail to software systems, and concentrate instead on decision-making with an IT input or on computer-aided design. Centralised information control with respect to overall business outcomes can coexist with decentralised decision-making and creativity.

The tornado comes from these three technological winds blowing together. Flexible process control technology offers a combination of economies of scale and customisation of product. But the communication of information and know-how means that others can utilise the product and control technologies for themselves within a very short time. So the development of a new product gives only short-term advantage. Once other organisations have the technology, the originator has no advantages in quality or costs. IBM and some Japanese organisations put less effort into original R&D than into developing others' ideas in this way.

So organisations in hi-tech manufacturing in particular are on a treadmill. They have to invest continually in leading-edge technology to gain a brief competitive advantage with new products. Any advantage in quality or cost will soon be wiped out by the transmission to others by technological means of their own technological advantage. They can't afford to ignore flexible control technology, since if they don't invest in it they'll suffer higher costs than their competitors. The same is true of service industries – which banks or supermarkets that don't invest in EFTPOS (Electronic Funds Transfer at Point of Sale) will survive? But such product flexibility and service convenience only serve to make customers more demanding. They want new, better and more individualised products and services, and they want them sooner. The life cycle of a product is so compressed that by comparison the mayfly might consider itself a long liver. And the requirement for speedy product development necessarily follows – creativity to order, and fast.

So the winds of change really are a tornado. All aspects of technological change – invention, process control, information storage and communication, decision and design modelling – interact. The demands of customers and the threat of the competition mandate a co-ordinated use of technology, which in its turn requires a profound organisational adaptation.

How have leading corporations adapted? Their strategies may be the pattern that others will follow in the next decade. Organisations have sought to win strategic advantages in the past

- by being particularly responsive to customers' and clients' needs;
- by being cost competitive;
- or by pioneering new products or services.

Now they are forced to compete on all three fronts simultaneously as a consequence primarily of technological change. How are they trying to do so? One strategy is to consciously strive to be transnational. Another is to focus the organisation on its *core competencies*, and co-ordinate and integrate its activities around them. And a third is to engage in mergers, acquisitions, and *alliances*, especially the latter. These strategies are not mutually exclusive – many world-class organisations consciously use all three.

Transnationalisation

First, becoming transnational. Bartlett and Ghoshal make some clear definitions for us, rooted in the historical development of several world-class organisations.[2] They distinguish multinational, global, international and transnational companies.

- A *multinational* is decentralised and nationally self-sufficient. It started as a national enterprise, and then gave a great deal of autonomy to its overseas offspring so that they could meet the different market needs of their new territory. Unilever and Philips have been multinationals.
- *Global* organisations have a highly centralised structure, with strategic control from the original country of origin. However, they market on a global scale, and seek for competitive advantage by economies of scale. McDonald's and Benetton are examples. Many Japanese organisations have developed in this way (Honda, for example).
- Bartlett and Ghoshal's third category, *international*, is halfway between multinational and global. The core know-how is developed and centred in the country of origin, but is exported and adapted abroad. So international companies have some of the local responsiveness of multinationals, and some of the economies of scale of global organisations. Many large American organisations fit this description – Procter and Gamble and ITT, for example.

However, the successful global, multinational and international organisations are nowadays beating their competitors by becoming *transnational*. In order to achieve economies of scale, *and* flexibility to local markets, *and* know-how dissemination, they are developing in entirely new ways. Each one of these objectives was achieved pre-eminently by one of the three types:

- global for economies of scale;
- multinational for flexibility;
- international for know-how dissemination.

Transnationals achieve all three simultaneously. They gain *economies of scale* by concentrating their main functions in a very few localities. So, for example, they may have two or three huge production facilities. One may be in the country of origin, but the siting of others will take advantage of, for example, a cheap labour market. Research and development similarly will be under one or two roofs, and will take advantage of local centres of know-how excellence. Transnationals obtain their *local flexibility* by the degree of specialisation which their subsidiaries can possess. And their *know-how* gets disseminated because the different national parts of the organisation are interdependent. The R&D people in the Netherlands have to deal with the producers in Italy and Wales.

One thing's for sure – becoming transnational requires the abandonment of any strongly nationally based management culture and values. The days of business imperialism are drawing to a close; everyone needs knowledge.

Core competencies

But what is the nature of this know-how? How can it conceivably be used on a worldwide scale? This is where our second strategic response mode comes in: the idea of corporate competencies (no relation to managerial competencies, which we consider in chapter 7).

As John Stopford insists,[3] organisations can't become transnational just by making acquisitions and mergers across international boundaries. The folly of the non-strategic acquisitions typical of the 70s was realised in the 80s, when many conglomerates found they were so diversified in products and markets that they weren't competing successfully in any of them. So they wisely divested, and as a consequence reduced the number of markets in which they operated. However, argues Stopford, this divestment was usually made on the basis of retaining those businesses which were profitable. It was not made on the basis of the identity of underlying core competencies. If it had been, these organisations would have found that their markets were increasing in number; for if an organisation's strategy is based on its core competencies, these will rapidly spawn new products and services, which will capture new markets.

So what is this corporate competence, this philosopher's stone allegedly capable of turning all into gold? In an article destined to become one of the classics of the business literature, C.K. Prahalad and Gary Hamel give us some answers.[4] Core competencies are 'the collective learning in the organisation'. How do you know when you've got one?

– if you have increased access to a range of markets;
– if it obviously contributes to customer benefit;
– and it's hard to imitate.

Individual technologies are easy to imitate – it's how knowledge is co-ordinated across the organisation that constitutes a competence. Organisations will have half a dozen such competencies at the most.

Prahalad and Hamel give as an example of a competence Philips' leadership in compact data storage and retrieval, which is a class of product functionality. They liken core competencies to the roots of a tree, the trunk and limbs of which are core products, the physical embodiments of core competences. The small electric motor at the heart of many of Black and Decker's products is such a core product. These core products are a precious possession – the organisation has to keep control of such critical components.

The businesses or divisions within an organisation or corporation are smaller branches, yielding particular leaves, flowers and fruits (specific products, such as a Black and Decker drill). So business units should not be the basic building blocks of the corporation, as they typically were in the 80s. Rather, more abstract competencies form the underlying logic from which strategy and co-ordination flow. So how do organisations succeed in going global on the basis of a relatively few core competencies? How does Canon successfully convert its competencies in optics, imaging, and microprocessor controls into copiers, laser printers, cameras and image scanners, all products which are leaders in their markets? Answer: they share know-how across the corporation; or they get it from elsewhere.

Sharing knowledge isn't as easy as it sounds. Successful companies design knowledge transfer into their organisational structure. They encourage and reward gurus, and prevent them from becoming the property of any one part of the corporation.

Prahalad and Hamel 'find it ironic that top management devotes so much attention to the capital budgeting process yet typically has no comparable mechanism for allocating the human skills that embody core competencies'. In companies such as Canon, specialists don't belong to this business or that division. They belong to the imaging fraternity (and sorority). Their know-how is transferred globally, in person or otherwise. And underlying the effective use of know-how are the power of information technology and the learning culture.

As Kim Clark notes, the key task for know-how organisations is to find the common ground between their technological knowledge and design, production, marketing and human resources.[5] It is this co-ordination capacity which forms core competencies. The adaptive properties of IT allow the whole of the product or service cycle to be responsive to changes in its subsystems. Indeed, it can incorporate supplier and retailer information, a capability which implies either very close co-operation or takeover.

So the identification of the core competencies of an organisation and their rapid dissemination can help the organisation compete globally. The concentration of resources into a relatively few competencies results in multiple products, since it is the same few core competencies which underlie diverse products. Hence there is greater speed in product development – a lot of the basic work has been done already; and there are economies of scale, as the same core product is at the heart of a variety of final products. Clearly, competencies are dependent on people with know-how, who will be expected to acquire it, keep it up to date, and pass it on.

Strategic alliances

But what happens when a core competence necessary for core products or their successful marketing and selling is not available? This is where the third form of organisational strategy comes in. Often accompanying globalisation and core competencies we have the formation of strategic alliances. Strategic alliances are ways of exchanging what you've already got for what you need. If your core competencies don't provide all the technological know-how on the core products you need, then you seek them elsewhere. Acquisition and joint ventures might carry risks. As Kenichi Ohmae notes,[6] many parents find that their offspring become a threat. Instead, arrangements of mutual benefit can be made between organisations which treat each other, at least ostensibly, as on an equal footing.

The need for cost competitiveness often makes alliances a way of saving on fixed costs:

- Where R&D, design, and production costs are high, it can be beneficial to share the distribution network of another company. Nissan and Volkswagen, Mazda and Ford, share distribution facilities; so do certain pharmaceuticals.
- Some semi-conductor manufacturers, for example Siemens and Philips, even contribute to shared R&D.
- Canon and Kodak exchange core products as components.
- Thomson and JVC actually engage in joint manufacture of video recorders.

All of these co-operative ventures save the partners time and money.

What makes for successful alliances? Gary Hamel and colleagues closely examined fifteen strategic alliances.[7] They found that alliances worked well when:

- each party has a clear objective in collaborating;
- each recognises the partner's objective as different from their own;

- each is clear what knowledge it should not surrender to the other;
- the parties don't compete in exactly the same market;
- they both have a bigger joint rival;
- they are contributing a core product or competence.

Japanese partners in strategic alliances have often come out of them with more favourable benefits than their partners. This may be because the contribution they usually have to make – a core competence in manufacturing excellence – is hard to transfer to another organisation. A core competence is a way of co-ordinating a process. It involves more than the transmission of a specific piece of technological knowledge. Japanese organisations, on the other hand, are often seeking precisely that: a piece of technological knowledge. They are looking for something more easily transferable, and so in principle are more likely to get what they want. Moreover, they are very good at listening and learning, but not always so eager to communicate. Western specialists will perhaps have to learn to be less forthcoming, and Western organisations will have to develop their competitor intelligence systems so that they know what they *could* get out of an alliance.

Lots of alliances don't work. Recent attempts by AT&T and Philips failed. Some are entered into by one of the parties out of a desperate need to survive. In others, one of the parties has given away too much of its core competencies, with the consequence that volume manufacturers gain brand dominance. In some cases the contributions of the parties were unequal in the first place. In others, suspicion grows that takeover rather than alliance is the real name of the game. The skills required to maintain an alliance will be in prime demand in the 90s.

In any case, too many alliances may be too much of a good thing. In recent research described in his book, *The Competitive Advantage of Nations*, Harvard Professor Michael Porter looked at a hundred companies in ten countries.[8] He found that nations were supreme in certain market segments rather than in markets as a whole: Germany excels in *luxury* cars, for example. And this national excellence was more likely to occur when there was strong competition within that segment in the same country – Audi, BMW and Mercedes. In other words, competition is good for you in the long run – keep taking the medicine.

So driven by the tornado of technological change, big corporations seek to achieve competitive advantage by building alliances, going transnational, and 'rethinking the concept of corporation' in terms of core competencies rather than strategic business units.[9]

But how typical of the next decade are these industrial giants? They all seem to be in manufacturing rather than services. They have all passed through those stages of development which many are only just entering. They are already large enough to ride the environmental threats which others desperately fight. Is it likely that medium-sized nationally based organisations will develop in the same way? Or are their markets and their products and services different in kind? I'll aim to show that while there may be some distinctions between multinationals and the rest, the same basic issues are around. If we look at the retail and the financial sectors as case studies, the same issues will hit us hard between the eyes – and these sectors are service rather than manufacturing, national more than multinational.

First let's consider three other environmental factors which we know now are going to happen: labour market shortages based on demographic and educational trends; the European legislation of 1992; and increased concern about our natural environment.

Demography and education

The basic demographic changes which affect the supply of labour are by now fairly well known. The number of UK school-leavers in the early and mid-90s is about two-thirds of what it was in the 80s, and this pattern is repeated in most northern and middle European countries. In the UK the education and training institutions are failing to develop these young people to anything like their intellectual potential. We will need to educate to a high level a greater number from this smaller population. The scientific and technological knowledge which is most needed is least forthcoming; the biggest shortfall in supply relative to demand is in graduates of these types. Broadening access to higher education isn't going to solve this problem – older and disadvantaged students tend to prefer arts and social science disciplines. Longer-term investment, if it occurs, will be too late for this decade. Morale in UK schools and universities is now so low and pay and conditions so poor that few good pure and applied scientists are attracted into teaching and research in the education sector.

So, given that the increases in labour market demand are in precisely those areas where supply is most lacking, the problem is more than demographic; it is also institutional and political. The changing nature of organisations means that less operatives, particularly in manufacturing and less administrative junior and middle managers will be needed. The British education and training system has never thrown off the elitist structures formalised in the 1944

Education Act. It will produce large numbers of young people who are not educated to be anything other than unskilled or semi-skilled operatives. And it still downgrades the application of science relative to the cultivation of the generalist. Without huge investment, the same state of affairs will continue into the twenty-first century; we can forget the rest of the twentieth.

It isn't just investment that's needed. As Douglas Hague points out,[10] the integration of education with people's adult development is vital. With knowledge becoming obsolescent at an ever-increasing rate, lifelong continuing education should be the agenda. And this doesn't mean more of the same – it means innovating in delivery methods and in objectives.

New knowledge will be imported by new technologies and at the learner's convenience; but how to be innovative, how to foster change, how to reflect imaginatively upon what one might do and how one might do it – these are the key objectives. All these things are decades away at present, held back by gross underfunding and by lack of a strategic educational vision.

1992 and all that

For those of us who are Europeans, this bleak picture ignores one of the effects of our second environmental change, however. In 1992 we will see the removal of barriers to the flows of goods, services, money, capital and, especially, *people*. Accreditation of professional qualifications across the European Community means that knowledge workers will be able to sell their labour wherever they wish. Of course, it is entirely another question whether the net flows will be into or away from the UK. With the economic centre moving inexorably to a reunited Germany, and with the UK dragging its feet, the probability is surely one of exodus from the UK rather than entry.

What of the other impacts upon organisations of 1992? Douglas Hague believes prices will be reasonably equal, markets reasonably free, and genuinely European financial institutions will open up possibilities for borrowing and lending on a far wider scale than at present. Gross national product in the EC as a whole may well rise by 5 per cent in the 90s, Hague estimates. Whether the UK achieves this average increase will, of course, depend on whether:

- government invests in infrastructure;
- industry and the City invests in development;
- and wage inflation is controlled.

Hague foresees a threat from Eastern Europe, where countries whose economies are still in the 1950s and 60s will be exporting mass-produced low- and medium-technology products. This is another reason for concentrating on high-technology manufacturing and service and a further impetus towards knowledge workers. Information technology isn't much use without the information.

One particular aspect of the EC which received short shrift in the UK during the 80s has been the *social dimension*: the policy of developing EC regulation of the labour market alongside the single market legislation of 1992. As Mark Hall points out,[11] EC employment law directives of the 70s affected UK practice. This influence was exerted both on specific practices, for example equal opportunity, but also via case law in the European Court of Justice. During the 1980s, however, the UK government fought every attempt to regulate the labour market. Partly as a consequence, the EC approach has moved away from specific legal instruments towards broad community-wide standards. This leaves individual member states some flexibility to implement EC initiatives according to their own situations. Yet it is clear that the main thrust of these initiatives is in terms of employees' rights, regarding equitable pay, atypical employment contracts, working time and, perhaps most significant, the information, consultation and participation of the employees.

In the European Company Statute, international and multinational companies are permitted a variety of different ways of ensuring participation, including worker representation on the board and the creation of a separate body of workers' representatives. In an era of increasing part-time employment and fixed-term employment contracts,[12] the provisions on atypical contracts are also very topical. Given that almost all the EC nations are more eager to implement the social dimension than is the UK, these developments are likely to have profound effects on UK organisations. They may find themselves at a disadvantage in the labour market since they will be offering less favourable employment contracts. Further, unless they are willing to match the European move towards participation, yet another cultural obstacle will be put in the way of multinational corporate cultures. Transatlantic corporations may well be successful in adapting to a European business culture; whether they can cope with fragmented employment practices is another matter.

Environmental issues

The third and final environmental factor affecting organisations in the 1990s is the environment itself. Specifically, it is clear that global warming will not be contained unless we slow down industrially based economic growth on a worldwide scale. Given that Eastern Europe, India, China and the USSR are currently moving into an era of increasing industrial development, the advanced economies of Europe, North America and the Pacific rim will have to slow down if the problem is to be solved.

It is another question, however, whether there is the political will to tackle the issue yet. We may see piecemeal measures such as charging car drivers for entering cities, but this will be because government ministers find themselves unable to get to meetings because of traffic jams! There is no sign of overall strategy, and it will take a long time for the groundswell of informed public opinion to enforce a political agenda. Hence a global issue which should be profoundly affecting the business climate of the 1990s is unlikely to do so till the twenty-first century. Hague therefore concludes that economic growth will continue as before in the 1990s,[13] with the Pacific rim in particular leading the way. But there is one way in which environment with a capital E will affect organisations. Knowledge workers may vote with their feet if their ecological values are not expressed in their organisation's culture, but more of that in chapter 4. My purpose in this chapter is to point up those business trends which affect what expectations organisations will hold of their employees.

Now for two case studies that clearly point to the existence of the key issues which we have already identified. The cases concern more nationally based non-manufacturing sectors: retail and finance.

Trends in retail

The retail sector in the UK and elsewhere has changed beyond all recognition. As Richard Ford puts it, 'Retailers have changed in the course of the 20th Century from places where producers show their products to places where consumers show their tastes.'[14] As the boundary between the manufacturer and the consumer, retailers have often forced improved quality upon the manufacturer on the consumer's behalf. A core competence of the retailer is to be able to *discover and react to the demands of the consumer*.

This usually involves identifying a market segment, a category of customer whose need the retailer is particularly well fitted to meet. Market segments differ in terms of the ratio of price to service they expect. A retail warehouse stacks its shelves from floor to ceiling with goods still in their cardboard boxes. It invites customers to pay for little more than the production, distribution and storage costs: help they certainly will not get. Nieman Marcus give each designer sweater five square metres of display space and will offer supremely tactful yet totally modish advice. The warehouse clientele pays for the product with hardly any service; the Nieman Marcus clientele for the service with hardly any product!

The successful discovery and exploration of a market segment is like the development and production of a new product. The design and style which captures a market segment for a retailer is soon imitated by competitors, just as a new product is imitated by other manufacturers. And just as with manufacturers, it is these new styles and designs, these newly discovered market segments, which are the main source of competitive advantage. This is because there is little competitive advantage to be gained in greater efficiency. Information technology has been embraced by all the leading retailers within a very short period. Its use is therefore a necessary but not a sufficient condition for competitive advantage. If you don't computerise your stock-taking and assess profits and sales of individual products, then you can't control your stock to allow just-in-time replenishment, nor your purchasing to reflect customer demand.

So the issues in retail are not dissimilar to those in manufacturing. You need information technology to be efficient and competitive, and to co-ordinate the purchase, distribution, storage, display and selling of goods. But you also need more than technology per se. It's the discovery of the consumer's preferences and tastes, and the use of this knowledge in defining a market segment and designing for it, which add value and which provide a distinctive competence.

The recent history of the retail industry suggests that not all retailers have this core competence. The present trend is for sales per square foot of space to decline in several retail sectors (for example, men's clothes). Shopping as a leisure pursuit, with a relatively high ratio of service to price and huge hypermarkets full of trendy boutiques, has recently been identified as attractive to a large segment of the consumer market. Perhaps this identification was premature. Perhaps the segment is much smaller than seemed likely in the heady days of the mid-80s. The point is that no amount of creative design of space and mood can compensate for faulty knowledge about how many people will want to be spaced out in this harmless way.

Another similarity with manufacturing industry is the need for economies of scale accompanied by local variations. The same retail organisation can aim for different market segments simultaneously – Marks & Spencer's clothes and food are an example. And individual stores can design innovatively for their local market, which may have, for example, a strong ethnic or generation flavour.

Economies of scale coupled with such local responsiveness are also facilitated by alliances, especially with manufacturers and distributors. So retail is like manufacturing:

- IT is a necessary condition for competitive advantage, but not a sufficient one.
- There are core retailing competencies.
- Knowledge and innovation give competitive edge.
- Alliances help improve cost competitiveness.
- Rapid responsiveness to the customer is vital.

What's not shared is the possibility of being gobbled up! Retail can never gobble up manufacturing, but the reverse may come true. Computer terminals linked to standard telephones (the MINITEL system) may permit the manufacturer to bypass the retailer in the long run.

Trends in the finance industry

Now for the finance industry. I took this sector as a case study because it wasn't manufacturing and because it was nationally rather than internationally based. But the latter assumption is becoming more outdated by the day. It was the entry of foreign banks into the UK banking system and the injection of international competition in the securities industry which triggered off the 1980s deregulation of the industry. The finance industry was transformed in the 1980s. As David Llewellyn describes so powerfully, specialist functional institutions gave way to conglomerates.[15] Commercial banking, investment banking, securities trading and portfolio management had each been the territory of separate institutions. Now single institutions could diversify into all these areas and a few others too. Conversely, any single service could be sold by a multitude of providers. So, for example, building societies have moved on from collecting savings to finance mortgages. They now lend money, provide insurance, broker stocks and shares, manage investments and transmit money. If you want a mortgage, you can get one from:

- a building society;
- a clearing bank;
- a foreign bank;
- an insurance company; or
- a specialist mortgage institution.

This *diversification* has enabled financial institutions to spread their risks. But, more important, it has opened them up to more *competition* from a wider variety of providers. So competition both triggered deregulation and resulted from it. As Llewellyn notes, the great rush to diversify in the late 1980s has brought its penalties. Sharp competition has meant that organisations have had to start rationalising their portfolio of businesses. Just as in manufacturing industry, the age of acquisitions has given way to the age of core competencies, so in the finance industry organisations are beginning to divest themselves of some hasty acquisitions. Insurance companies have been getting rid of estate agencies like hot potatoes. What's more, the huge cultural incompatibility of high risk-taking extroverted merchant bankers with solid and sober retail bankers has led to a few marital bust-ups.

As with manufacturing and retail, information technology is a necessary but not a sufficient condition for competitive advantage in financial services. As in manufacturing, IT actually makes new products available. For example, insurance salespeople can now visit clients, discover their financial circumstances, feed these into an expert system in their lap-top computer, and come up with a personal plan there and then. Furthermore, IT increases the efficiency of existing services, so that there are few cost efficiency advantages to be gained in basic services. For example, the costs of transactions in financial markets have been considerably reduced. As Amin Rajan has noted,[16] this has spurred the development of financial innovations, in the form of new service products which can be customised to clients' requirements.

The *communication* advantages of IT mean that domestically the customer doesn't have to be physically close to a branch for some services, as First Direct has demonstrated. Internationally it makes it just as easy for overseas suppliers of financial services to compete for custom as for domestic suppliers. Communication between the international finance centres can also be immediate and full. The modelling capacities of IT permit immediate calculation of risks and rapid response to lending requests. So, to sum up on technology, 'changes in the economic and financial environment may have created a demand for new instruments, (financial products) but the development of technology has enabled these demands to be met'.[17]

The consequences are the same as in manufacturing and retail. Competitive advantage comes from new products geared to market segments rather than from cost competitiveness on its own. Hence innovative products created by knowledge workers are the key to success, and *the acquisition, development, and retention of know-*

how is a key issue. However, organisations have first to identify what their core competencies are, and base their corporate strategy upon such an analysis.

A transnational strategy is also a necessity despite strongly domestic corporate histories. Apart from the ease of international dealing resulting from IT, the new financial products, such as futures and options, operate across markets and financial centres. What's more, overseas competitors can muscle in successfully on domestic markets since they don't suffer from greater transaction costs or lack of access to customers. Such a capacity to enter domestic markets is one of the elements of becoming global. Domestic financial institutions therefore face a hard competitive struggle at home, and, if they are late to internationalise, will find it difficult to compete globally too. They face exactly the same strategic dilemma as their manufacturing and retail colleagues. How can they both decentralise decision-making so as to permit creativity and flexible response to local demand, and at the same time devise a corporate strategy which develops core competencies as the only way to achieve competitive advantage?

We can sum up the business trends of the next decade as follows: most of them could probably have been written at the start of the 80s as well:

- greater competition for larger and freer markets;
- increased use of technology in every organisational function;
- identification and investigation of market segments;
- rapid development and manufacture of new market-led products and services;
- customisation of products and services from a common base;
- decentralised decision-making in line with central corporate strategy;
- greater integration of functions by means of information technology;
- increased internationalisation and globalisation;
- more alliances, takeovers and divestments.

All of these business trends require the identification and development of core organisational competencies, and the treatment of knowledge as the key organisational asset. What will organisations expect of their employees when they are faced with these business imperatives?

Some final questions

About your own career

- Which of the above nine business trends have most affected your career in the last five years? How has each trend affected it?
- Which trends do you expect will have most impact on your career over the next five years? How will each affect it?
- What are the core competencies of your organisation? With which of these have you been most involved? How has this involvement affected your career?

About your organisation

- Is your organisation in the process of becoming international? multinational? transnational? How has this affected the way it manages careers?
- Does it intend to expand organically, or by acquisition, or both? How is this affecting the way it manages careers?
- Or is it contracting? What effects on careers will this have? How will it cope with them – and how will *you* cope with them?
- What effects will 1992 have on your organisation's management of careers?
- What sector-specific factors will affect your organisation, and how will it cope with them?

Notes

1 K. Clark (1989) 'What strategy can do for technology', *Harvard Business Review*, 89 (6): 94–8.

2 C.A. Bartlett and S. Ghoshal (1989) *Managing Across Borders*. Hutchinson: London.

3 J. Stopford (1990) 'Whatever happened to the Euro-multinational?', *Issues*, 10: 12–17.

4 C.K. Prahalad and G. Hamel (1990) 'The core competence of the corporation', *Harvard Business Review*, 90 (3): 79–91.

5 Clark, op. cit.

6 K. Ohmae (1989) 'The global logic of strategic alliances', *Harvard Business Review*, 89 (2): 143–54.

7 G. Hamel, Y.L. Doz and C.K. Prahalad (1989) 'Collaborate with competitors and win', *Harvard Business Review*, 89 (1): 133–9.

8 M. Porter (1990) *The Competitive Advantage of Nations*. New York: Free Press.

9 Prahalad and Hamel, op. cit.

10 D. Hague (1990) 'The business environment of the 1990s', paper delivered at the Association for Management Education and Development Conference, Stratford-upon-Avon.

11 M. Hall (1990) 'UK employment practices after the social charter', *Personnel Management*, March: 32–5.

12 R.S. Williams (1989) 'Patterns of employment and the job market', in P. Herriot (ed.), *Assessment and Selection in Organisations*. Chichester: John Wiley.

13 Hague, op. cit.

14 R. Ford (1990) 'Managing retail service businesses for the 1990s: marketing aspects', *European Management Journal*, 8 (1): 58–62.

15 D.T. Llewellyn (1990) 'Structural change in the British financial system', in C. Green and D.T. Llewellyn (eds), *Surveys in Monetary Economics*, vol. 2. Oxford: Blackwell.

16 A. Rajan (1988) 'Today the city, tomorrow . . . Managing a knowledge economy', *Personnel Management*, October: 30–7.

17 D.T. Llewellyn (1985) *Evolution of the British Financial System*. London: Institute of Bankers, p.12.

3

Starship Enterprise

Kirk the adventurous

International competitiveness; technological change; product obsolescence; decentralisation but core competencies; alliances, takeovers and divestments – a cascade of change, forcing organisations to make ever increasing demands on their employees. The major categories of these demands are as follows; their connections with business trends are immediately obvious:

- to pilot organisational change, and to become international in outlook;
- to remain loyal and committed to the organisation throughout;
- to keep one's knowledge up to date and to be innovative;
- to accept responsibility for meeting customers' needs and to report market trends.

These expectations may all fall upon the broad shoulders of one poor soul. An international marketing manager whose expertise is in the area of information technology might be an example. More likely, one or two of the four will impinge strongly upon any one individual:

- the chief executive of a subsidiary business might primarily face the first and third expectations;
- a long-serving sales supervisor the second and fourth;
- a medical laboratory scientist the second and third;
- a systems analyst the third;
- a tele-sales person the fourth.

So what is expected depends on who one is. But the organisation's expectations will also depend on its own position. How is it reacting to the current business trends, and what position did it start from? Organisations have different strategies for coping with their environment, and different strategic approaches involve different weight being given to certain of their expectations. More of this later. For now, we'll concentrate on each of the four categories of expectations and give each an icon. And what more appropriate icon than that archetype of futuristic adventure – *Starship Enterprise*.

As *Starship Enterprise* charts its course through the 90s, what will it expect of its crew? It can't do without the indispensable Captain Kirk for a start. In the 90s, organisations will want people to boldly go where no man has gone before – all the way across the Channel, for example. Several of the business trends of the 90s imply the need for intrepid travellers – travellers not just through space, but through cultures.

Internationalisation obviously requires the willingness to be mobile physically, with all that this implies for disruption to personal, family and social life. But it also means leaving the safe anchorage of one's own national and organisational culture. In the last chapter we noted that Western organisations had tended to internationalise in a diversified manner. They often acquired local businesses and encouraged them to keep their own culture, believing it likely to be suited to the national culture in which it was rooted. UK managers going abroad consequently can't even rely on familiarity with at least one part of the culture shock that hits them – the culture of their own organisation. On the contrary, they may be required to perform a functional role (marketing manager) in an utterly different organisation; or they may have been given the task of turning around a badly managed local branch.

But of course, going abroad to manage one of the corporation's businesses isn't the whole story. Alliances and takeovers, but especially the former, will increase in number during the 90s. These territories require yet more delicate exploration. Captain Kirk's past practice has been to approach the representatives of other organisations head on at a vast rate of knots, and zap them if they don't get out of the way. The conduct of alliances is bit more subtle. The skills involved are those of negotiation and communication, and both are notoriously difficult across organisational and national cultural boundaries. We only have to watch northern Europeans failing to haggle in Eastern food markets and treating the whole episode as really rather distasteful. But alliances are a special case – they need hard-headed negotiation about what the parties will get from each other, then the communication of just that and no more. Westerners happily gush away about their really interesting work; Japanese listen.

It is easy to trivialise cultural differences, to try to reduce them to different social behaviour. We all know by now of the Arab–English *pas de deux*, caused by differences in preferred physical distance from the other person. Arabs prefer a smaller distance, and hence advance on retreating Brits desperate to keep their own distance. But it's in underlying values and assumptions that the important differences lie. What are these key differences across cultures, and how will the Captain Kirk of the 90s be expected to cope with them?

We will start with some very basic assumptions that differ, move on to differences in values, and finish up with the varieties of meanings given to work. Note that cultures and nations are not synonymous: some cultures may cross nations (for example Latin America), others divide them (for example French and Anglo-Canadian).

E.S. and C.G. Glenn point up some very fundamental differences in assumptions between different cultures.[1] What has greater significance in a culture, ask the Glenns: what people do, who they are, or what they say? We are used to paying lots of attention to what people do, and when we need to know more we look them up in *Who's Who*, where we find a list of their achievements. Southern Europeans, on the other hand, are much less oriented towards action – they are more concerned with relationships. How is the other person disposed towards me, how reciprocal are they likely to be if I do them a favour? Other cultures, again, pay more attention to what's said. Words, for them, speak louder than actions, and have to express ideological nuances exactly. This is why Kremlinologists and sinologists are great textual critics – as, indeed, are Russian and Chinese people themselves.

A second major difference in assumptions is about process versus goal. In some cultures, people are future oriented and devise ways of achieving long-term goals; in others they concentrate on the present and how best to live it.

The final distinction which the Glenns make is between ways of processing information. In some cultures, information is processed in the abstract. It doesn't need to come in any particular form – it may be through various electronic media, the press, or through memos, papers and so on. The context of the transmission of the information is unimportant, and as a consequence it is dealt with in a factual, analytic way. For others, the context really matters. Who is providing the information, are they telling us face to face, and what is the nature and current mood of the relationship between us? In general, transatlantic and northern European countries follow the former processing mode; Greece, Spain, China and Japan the latter.

These seem very abstract differences indeed. But it is this very generality which results in their expression in a multitude of different settings and behaviours. So in southern European countries, which are people oriented, much more organisational attention and time will be spent in establishing interpersonal relationships, since they are people rather than action oriented. Go to a Silicon Valley hi-tech consultancy, on the other hand, and all you have to do is tell them which projects you've managed. Speak with a Russian or Chinese with care – they are weighing your words, and expect you to weigh theirs!

Concentration on process as opposed to goals similarly has profound implications for organisational culture: many oriental organisations have strong and detailed rules about how people should deal with internal and external clients; yet management by objectives wouldn't have caught on in China as it did in the West.

Finally, the more organisations depend on know-how, the more cultural differences in ways of communicating it become important: face to face or fax to fax.

Geert Hofstede has discovered a tremendous amount about differences in *values* across cultures.[2] From a huge survey spanning forty countries using 88,000 employees of a single multinational firm, Hofstede came up with four value dimensions along which they differ. Some cultures have individualistic values, placing much more importance on the individual than the collective. The USA has the most individualistic values of any country, and Mrs Thatcher tried to induce a value shift in that direction in the UK. The organisational practices which reflect such values are, for example, rewards based on individual rather than team performance.

Hofstede's second crucial value dimension was that of power. How great is the difference in power between the lower and the higher members of the organisational hierarchy? Again, rewards and privileges and opportunities are outward and visible signs of the power distance between organisational levels. As Charles Handy has often pointed out,[3] organisational cultures based on power imply very different relationships between people and ways of taking decisions than cultures based, for example, on know-how.

The third important value dimension identified by Hofstede is that of uncertainty. Some cultures avoid uncertainty like the plague. They try to control it by explicit rules and structures, and by acceptance of the goals set by the senior management of the organisation. One country which especially dislikes uncertainty and seeks to control it is Japan. Given the uncertainty of the business environment in the 90s, one would have thought that the Japanese would be at a disadvantage. Some Pacific rim countries (such as Hong Kong and Singapore) are tolerant of ambiguity and uncertainty, however.

Masculinity is Hofstede's final value dimension. This refers to assertiveness and preference for material rewards as opposed to co-operation and preference for quality-of-life rewards. Highly masculine values imply certain beliefs about what motivates people, and will again be reflected in reward and career systems and in the ways in which people relate to each other at work.

Even though Hofstede's data were collected twenty years ago from a single organisation, they are the best basis we have at present for thinking about cross-national differences. But what about work itself? What meaning does it have for people, and how central is it in their lives? *The Meaning of Work Study*[4] asked this question of eight countries: the USA, Japan, the UK, West Germany, Belgium, Netherlands, Israel and Yugoslavia. Four basic patterns emerged from the research:

- There are some people for whom work isn't central in their lives, but the income they get from it is.
- For others, the reverse is true – work is very central, and a way of expressing themselves, but income doesn't matter so much.
- A third group feels they have a right to work, and value it for the social contact it gives them.
- A fourth group believes that work is more of an obligation than a right.

These four different patterns of meaning were expressed evenly within some countries (Belgium and the Netherlands). In Israel and Japan more people fell into the second group – high work centrality – than into the other three groups. In the USA and Yugoslavia more believed that work was an obligation more than a right. Clearly, to those who live to work and those who work to live, we need to add those who work to work! It says much for the centrality of work in our lives that the fourth category, living to live, isn't very prominent in our thinking.

It is into this only recently charted international mind-space that our intrepid Captain Kirk of the 90s will be expected to venture. He or she will run appalling risks if they boldly go encased in the cockpit of their own national and organisational culture. They have to own it but stand outside it – taking the metaphor to its ridiculous conclusion, they need to ride on the *Enterprise's* wing-tip! It is only when we stand on the outside of our cultural identity and look in through the windows that we can contemplate the idea that there are other equally valid ways of construing selves and society. One way of looking through our own window is to take notice of how others see us. Cartoons in continental European newspapers, for example, suggest that xenophobia is considered a national characteristic of the British.

We must conclude that the business trends of the 90s of inter-nationalisation and globalisation, of alliances and mergers, will result in organisations expecting profound personal changes of their employees. We will all have to become cultural relativists. We will have to be so secure in, and aware of, our own cultural identities that we can agree that they may be suitable for us but not for everyone; and we will have to respect other cultures' basic assumptions and values as being suitable for them. Hardest of all, we'll have to work out the implications of such basic differences for doing business with people. The statement 'He's a man I can do business with' might have had more implications than its speaker was aware of. The effects of culture on business relationships are indeed profound. Most of the classical prescriptions about managerial principles which we blithely thought were universally applicable are simply irrelevant in a multicultural environment. To take some of Fayol's five elements of management (planning, organisation, command, co-ordination and control):[5]

- How can we examine the future and draw up a *plan* of action when some of us believe plans are things we stick to through thick and thin in order to reduce uncertainty; others think they are temporary ways of making sense of where we're at; and others still perceive them as mere words with which it is appropriate to agree?
- How can we *co-ordinate* ('bind together, unify, and harmonise all activity and effort'), when some of us believe that individual rather than collaborative effort should be rewarded, and that business units within a corporation work best when pitted against each other?
- How can we *control* ('see that everything occurs in conformity with established rule and expressed command'), when some of us don't believe that this is a role function of managers at all, while others do it by the merest social gesture and assertion of status?
- How can we successfully *negotiate* about any of these managerial functions when some of us don't believe what people say until they demonstrate it by their actions; others only believe what the top person says; and others again only believe it when it's said in a certain way?

Managing becomes difficult indeed when the pit-props are knocked away. But dealing with other cultures is, of course, only one of the aspects of change facing employees. They will also be expected to take on the task of carrying through strategic changes, such as:

- moving from operating in one market to operating in several;
- adapting their culture to that of a major new acquisition;

- knocking out several managerial layers;
- devolving managerial and budgetary responsibility way down the line;
- working in project teams away from one's functional boss.

And so on, All of these profound organisational changes require learning and development, with which, as we shall see in chapter 7, employees will expect help and support.

Scotty the loyal

But Kirk needs his crew. Where would *Starship Enterprise* be without the stalwart Scotty, who reliably responds to the mysterious request 'Beam me up, Scotty'? Organisations depend in times of change on their solid citizens to give continuity and hold the whole thing together. There's a dynamic tension between adaptation to the environment and maintenance of the fabric of the organisation. Because they know it inside out, the Scotties of the organisational world can keep things going. They have served their time in the organisation and acquired a lot of inside knowledge. When others are busy plotting acquisitions or researching a new product, they can be relied upon to make sure that salaries are paid on time and that the unions are happy.

Scotties are also expected to be loyal in the sense of not succumbing to alien temptations. Kirk and Scotty have both been led astray in the past by the siren voices of other planets. In an era of increasing competitiveness and with more and more attention being paid to competitor information, Scotties can sometimes be a prize for rivals. They are particularly valuable if they've been around the organisation long enough to know how a particular core competence works. On the other hand, many Scotties have been so loyal in the past that they've done a whole range of jobs at the organisation's request. They've got no up-to-date expert knowledge to sell, and are often at the organisation's mercy. When layers of middle management are stripped away and they have the good fortune to survive, they're asked to be committed and work twice as hard.

Spock the egghead

How different from the next of our *Starship* characters, he of the pointy ears, Mr Spock. His loyalty often has to be bought. One UK organisation regularly trains its systems people in IT languages they will never use in the organisation; it does so in order to retain them by giving them the opportunity to keep completely up to date. The organisation, paradoxically, is having to increase their employability in order to retain their employment, as Kanter puts it.[6] And retaining them is crucial; first, because know-how is usually scarce; and secondly because they are the most likely to understand the core competencies which must not be given away.

What organisations will expect above all from its Spocks are up-to-date knowledge and its innovatory use. In order to maintain and develop its core competencies, organisations need knowledge workers. Given the key role of information technology in integrating the processes of production and co-ordinating them with supply, design, marketing and sales, all knowledge workers and managers will have to be IT literate. So not only will Spock's specific expertise need to be updated, he must continuously broaden his understanding of the implications of IT. As Eric Sveiby and Tom Lloyd argue; because there is only one asset worth anything – the people – the only way to develop a know-how company is to develop the people.[7]

The development and learning expected of people in the next decade is phenomenal. One cutting-edge British pharmaceutical company doesn't now recruit its scientists by their discipline. It recognises that the knowledge base is changing so fast that what is currently incorporated within one academic label will not be relevant in five years' time. As a consequence, it recruits on the criterion of ability to learn new things.

But keeping up to date won't be Spock's only responsibility. He'll have to be able to communicate his knowledge to others in that painfully logical style of his. There are two reasons for this. First, the essence of core competencies is that the knowledge upon which they are based is disseminated across the organisation. If the knowledge is in the heads of its Spocks, then they will have to make sure non-Spocks understand it. Secondly, the speed of product obsolescence means that the research and development, design, and manufacturing of new products will have to be streamlined. Instead of passing through the hands and heads of a series of groups of specialists, different specialists will collaborate in product teams. Spocks have to communicate with their distant relatives and even with other species. And they have to work with them.

What's more, they will have to have an understanding of the organisation's business, for their innovations have to meet or create a customer need. It's fine to have wacky hi-tech ideas, but if they don't result in a marketable core product derived from a core competence then they aren't going to be seen as relevant. This may be short-sighted – where, we may ask, are new core competencies going to come from? – but it reflects the commercial constraints of the 90s.

So Mr Spock will have to broaden his horizons. Like Scotty, he will have to take more responsibility, in his case for his own development. He cannot rely on a fast-track scheme which speeds him on a guided tour through the organisational galaxy before he takes up his senior position in *Starship Enterprise*. And he will have to appreciate that he cannot spout forth indigestible knowledge which totally baffles the rest of the crew.

Uhura at the sharp end

The eyes and ears of the *Enterprise* are Lieutenant Uhura, who warns efficiently of the rapid approach of unidentified objects. To emphasise her function, she always has a large plastic object sticking out of her ear.

Two of the key business trends of the 90s are the identification and investigation of market segments, and the customisation of products and services from a common base. Both require getting the right information from the environment and its intelligent use. In addition, the trend towards keener competition makes knowledge about one's competitors more important. Moreover, internationalisation makes global social, political and economic information indispensable, while at the other end of the scale, decentralisation means that local knowledge of markets results in local innovations and competitive advantage.

In his classic study of managerial work, Henry Mintzberg includes the role of *monitor* of information as one of the ten key roles the manager plays.[8] He found that managers prefer information about outside events and people more than about ideas or trends in the environment. Much of their information is not documented and originates from personal contacts in their networks. He also suggests that the more senior the manager, the greater part of their time is spent in this role.

This won't do for the 90s (Mintzberg was writing in 1973). *Every* employee will be expected to be the eyes and ears of the organisation, not just senior managers. And environmental scanning will be systematic and anticipatory of opportunities and threats, rather than reactive to chance information. Analysis of the environment will involve identifying important sectors of the environment and systematically monitoring them. It is far easier than diagnosis, which draws conclusions about the likely results of external environmental change. Predicting the effects of change is not as simple as recognising that change may occur.[9]

Environmental scanning means methodically scanning the environment for specific information which will help the company gain competitive advantage or achieve some desired future. Since much of the most valuable information is about clients or customers, employees who deal directly with them have a crucial role to play in environmental scanning. Only they can discover not merely that customers are buying less of a particular product or service, but why they are doing so. Only they know what it is that customers are asking for which they cannot provide at present.

So all employees of the 90s will have to obtain evidence actively from their environment. They will only know what evidence to get if they understand what it's going to be used for; and if they themselves actually want to achieve competitive advantage and/or satisfy the customer's needs. And they will have to infer the likely consequences from this information and the strategic issues they raise. Many organisations have been made forcibly aware of the demographic trough of the 90s. But how many have worked out its implications for their human resource strategy in advance? And how many will be able to move smoothly into the new recruitment systems, varied employment contracts, and redesigned training schemes which new types of employee will require? A recent survey found that more than half had no plans at all.[10]

The identification of market segments will be one of Uhura's responsibilities. The other will be tailoring the service she provides to the local and specific needs of the customer. There are few products and services which are the same all over their market; most vary to meet local tastes. Discovering those tastes and finding new ways to cater for them is Uhura's second task. She will require all her intelligence to find out what customers want and be innovative in her responses. And she'll need to be given the discretion to act accordingly. Organisations will expect her to take more and more responsibility; they'll give her control over her own budget, and power to take decisions. Whether they'll trust her with them is another matter.

If the overall mission is clear and accepted and the core competencies are well known, then they should leave her to it. The classic historical examples are the British colonial administrators of the nineteenth century and the Jesuit missionaries to the Americas; in both cases, the centre was confident that those at the cutting edge could be left to achieve the mission in their own way. Henry Mintzberg calls such organisations missionary organisations, with good reason.[11] But they both realised the importance of their front-line troops, and trained and developed them accordingly.

So the business trends of the 90s will lead to huge expectations by the organisation of the employees. *Starship Enterprise* has a crew – each plays a necessary role: Kirk the intrepid explorer, Scotty the loyal retainer, Spock the know-how man, and Uhura the eyes and ears. But many employees of the 90s will be expected to be all four rolled into one – international, loyal, learning and observant. And there's the rub. Not only is this an incredible burden of expectations to bear – it is also a contradictory one. How can the organisation realistically hope that an international manager won't 'go native'? How can it believe that an eminently marketable expert won't move on? How can it expect a top-level physicist to be bothered about the tastes of Joe Public? Distance and domesticity, learning and loyalty, maestros and markets – these are hard to reconcile.

After all, organisations haven't helped employees to meet these expectations in the 90s. The stripping away of layers of middle management and their subsequent 'outplacement' hasn't exactly earned reciprocal loyalty. The 80s emphasis on immediate individual performance and its individual reward hasn't actively encouraged teamwork and longer-term self-development. A decade of UK governmental ambivalence about Europe hasn't made things any easier for international organisations or managers.

The expectations of organisations for the 90s may be burdensome and demanding; they may seem incompatible with each other and with the practices of the previous decade. But even more important is the key career question – how compatible are they with people's expectations for themselves?

Some final questions

About your own career

- Which set of expectations – those of Kirk, Scotty, Spock or Uhura – do you feel most strongly? Which next?
- Which features of these expectations do you find it hardest to meet? Why?
- What international experience have you had? What did you learn from it? Has it helped your career? How were you prepared for it? Was the preparation adequate?
- How long have you been with your present organisation? Have you had the chance to leave? What kept you loyal?
- Would you describe yourself as a specialist or a generalist? Which of these two categories is more likely to have the opportunity for changing employer?

About your organisation

- To which of the four types of expectation does your organisation attach greater weight? Why do you think this is so? To which do you think it should be giving greatest weight? Why?
- Is your organisation global, multinational, international or national? In which ways has it changed its career policies as a result?
- Has your organisation reduced the number of managerial levels recently? What have been the consequences for long-serving employees? Do you foresee more such delayering in the future?
- Does your organisation form product development or other project groups consisting of a mix of specialists? How well do they work together? What are the main problems?
- Has your organisation devolved budgetary responsibilities recently? What other powers has it devolved? How does it get feedback from the customer interface? Is its method of doing so effective?

Notes

1 E.S. Glenn and C.G. Glenn (1981) *Man and Mankind*. Norwood, NJ: Ablex.

2 G. Hofstede (1980) *Culture's Consequences: International Differences in Work Related Values*. Beverley Hills, CA: Sage Publications.

3 C. Handy (1985) *Understanding Organisations*, 3rd edn. Harmondsworth: Penguin.

4 The Meaning of Work International Research Team (1987) *The Meaning of Working*. New York: Academic Press.

5 D.S. Pugh, D.J. Hickson and C.R. Hinings (1971) *Writers on Organisations*, 2nd edn. Harmondsworth: Penguin.

6 R.M. Kanter (1989) 'The new managerial work', *Harvard Business Review*, 89 (6): 85–92.

7 I.E. Sveiby and T. Lloyd (1987) *Managing Know-how*. London: Bloomsbury.

8 H. Mintzberg (1973) *The Nature of Managerial Work*. New York: Harper & Row.

9 W.J. Rothwell and H.C. Kazanas (1989) *Strategic Human Resource Development*. Englewood Cliffs, NJ: Prentice-Hall, p.114.

10 *The Impact of Age upon Employment* (Warwick Papers in Industrial Relations no.33). Industrial Relations Research Unit, Warwick University.

11 H. Mintzberg (1979) *The Structuring of Organisations*. Englewood Cliffs, NJ: Prentice-Hall.

Appendix

A week in the diary of an international manager, November 1990

5 November   London. Seminar on 'The Learning Organisation'. Emphasis on consultancy and management development in the international context. Lots of interest, but a methodology needed – too much theorising. Wide range of countries represented, especially Scandinavians, and many multinational organisations.

6 November   In office. a.m.: Visit from PM from south of France. Possibility of collaboration with PM to set up a project located in France but serving a general European market. a.m.: Visit from J.O. from Czechoslovakia – had met him at a conference two weeks ago. He was visiting UK funded by the British Council, to look at potential partnerships with UK organisations. He found us entirely compatible with his needs; but where's the mutual interest? Can they afford us? Worth running a seminar in Prague to keep our name prominent, though no immediate revenue to be expected. The Czech concept of quality and service are very different from ours, but once their minds are free I can't see any cultural differences getting in the way. p.m.: Meet with C.H.R. (colleague) for a briefing meeting preparing for our presentation on Thursday in Copenhagen. At 17.20 hours Gatwick to Paris. Meet G.B. (colleague) there. He had gone ahead a day in advance to prepare the meeting with the French in detail. I'm the door opener and flag waver, G.B. is a specialist on the French business scene. Dinner in Paris with the French director of PC (our parent company).

7 November   To Paris office of PC, our agents in France. Our fourth visit – the crunch presentation. They are making their business plans for next year and we want them to use our product. We'll help them finance the local development. Rehearsal of presentation from 10.00–12.00 hours (a Frenchman is the pretend audience) real presentation at 12.00 hrs. We promise sustained growth and high profitability despite recession. G.B. handles the heart-to-heart individual chats in French, though the presentation itself was in English. Unreserved commitment to our product. Lunch, then to airport with G.B. He goes to Brussels, I to Copenhagen, arrive 17.00 hrs. P.L. (colleague) arrives later for dinner, having spent a day in Copenhagen. C.H.R. (colleague) arrives from UK for tomorrow's presentation.

8 November   A month ago only 10 attenders promised, but 20 warm clients arrive. Introduction in Danish, presentation in English, 1.5 hours. Lots of penetrating questions: how international is our staff, for example. I mentioned G.M. (Irish). They laughed. Memo: must ensure that we recruit more international staff. P.L. and C.H.R. go off to Aarhus, to follow up a contact made at the presentation (a large specialist hi-tech organisation). Back to UK.

9 November   Work at home. Report writing and reflection, and catch up on admin. and planning. Think back on some cultural differences: one minor, one major. Why weren't we offered coffee when we arrived at the Paris office? Immediate reaction was 'They're not looking after us very well'. Answer: they go out for coffee to a coffee shop! And a major difference between France and Scandinavia – the French are primarily concerned about what's happening in the French regions: Marseilles, Lyons, Grenoble. The Scandinavians are truly international – they seek an international angle in every piece of business. Where are we? Is our international strategy truly integrated with our business strategy as a whole? We, as a company, seem half-way between the French and the Scandinavians.

4

Other Hats

Now that we've identified the need for Kirk, Scotty, Spock and Uhura, the next logical step is to discover how to get hold of them and weld them into an effective crew. But that's the organisation's logic. Following that logic, we'd be spending the present chapter on recruitment, induction, training and development, succession planning, rewards and compensation: all the career management systems designed to assist the organisation in achieving its objectives. That's not the logic of this book, for it is a limited and one-sided logic only. To get a full picture we have to progress up from the bottom of Figure 1.2 as well as down from the top. We have to look at the career enhancement of the employee as well as at career management by the organisation. We have to consider what people bring to the party.

The crew of the *Enterprise* look purposeful and efficient kitted out in their space helmets. But individuals come to organisations wearing all sorts of different hats in the real world. And each of these hats prompts them to hold various expectations about how the organisation should act. Employees don't leave their identities at home when they come to work; they bring their values with them. They come not only as employees and workers; they may also be citizens and professionals. Above all, they are unique individuals with their own histories and aspirations – with their own careers, and their own expectations of the organisation. The enormity of the organisation's demands will be matched in the 90s by the ever more discriminating and varied requirements of their employees.

Citizens

The first guise in which modern employees present themselves is as John or Jane Bull with an additional touch of the Ralph Naders. Employees are citizens. They bring with them various expectations about how the organisation should act in a socially responsible way. A major concern is that it should respect people's rights – people both outside and inside the organisation. Employees have no hesitation in construing their organisation as a moral agent. It can make contracts, be held responsible for its actions, and be accountable for their consequences. Milton Friedman's argument that 'The social responsibility of business is to increase profits' is only half of the truth as far as they are concerned.[1] And a corollary is that they as employees should not be expected to behave in ways that violate their own ethical standards.

Concern about the rights of the individual is currently a topic of great and growing importance. The UK is the only state in the Council of Europe which has no written constitution or enforceable Bill of Rights. In case after recent case, the European Court has supported weak individuals in the UK such as immigrants, prisoners and mental patients; and it has placed curbs on the powerful who seek to infringe their rights – police, prison administrators, courts. And, as we saw in chapter 2, the European social charter seeks to extend individual's rights, especially in the workplace. Equitable treatment regarding pay, working time, privacy, discrimination and disciplinary procedures are to be guaranteed. But even more important, the political principle of participating democracy is to be extended to the place of work. The organisation isn't seen just as a place of work, it isn't only a moral agent; it is also a community, in which members have rights and responsibilities. The flip side of employee commitment is corporate community.

These are big claims. How do we know that people are thinking this way about organisations? What indications are there that there is a public inclination to hold organisations responsible? Public response to recent events and issues has been strong and clear. Environmental issues in particular have given us a testing ground for public opinion, and organisations will ignore the public response at their peril. People blame organisational systems as well as individual fallibility for disasters such as Bhopal, Exxon Valdes and Chernobyl. And they certainly criticise organisations and governments who are mean and tardy in their reaction once the disaster has occurred. Wherever they can, the informed public is changing its patterns of consumption in order to try to ameliorate such problems as the depletion of the ozone layer and of the tropical rainforest, acid rain and oceanic pollution. The more committed form pressure groups, and special interest lobbies already have a major impact on domestic politics in the USA; they are becoming more influential in the UK.

But it is not just for environmental issues that the public holds organisations responsible. A whole raft of recent well-publicised events has put more pressure upon them. Take a series of UK accidents. The general public and indeed the victims themselves by and large felt that the *Herald of Free Enterprise* disaster was the responsibility of the company more than of the crew. Pressures of work, outdated systems, and attempts at cost control rather than individual carelessness were believed to underlie the various train crashes of the last two or three years. And even revelations that airline maintenance records were falsified in order to keep up with demanding schedules aren't merely individual misdemeanours.

People are concerned about standards of truthfulness in advertising, and its targeting of easily persuadable groups. While many blamed individuals for getting into debt when interest rates went up, many also questioned the ways in which easy credit facilities have been touted. They worry about the catastrophic consequences for employees of hostile takeovers. They are highly cynical about organisations' capacity to regulate and control their own storm-troopers – witness Guinness and Boesky. Even public sector service organisations now fail to enjoy the same esteem in which they have traditionally been held. The police and the judiciary have come very badly out of a series of recent cases in which there have been miscarriages of justice. People are not necessarily asking for a return to nanny state; but they *are* starting to hold organisations accountable for a variety of bad outcomes.

We can see why the public rightly holds organisations largely responsible. To go back to the culture metaphor (see pp. 10–11), the artifacts of organisational cultures point only too clearly to the underlying values which promote such outcomes. Take reward systems. If individual performance in achieving bottom-line financial profit is the sole or the major criterion for reward, then other consequences of actions will be devalued. Or take deadlines and schedules. If the meeting of the deadline is more important than the quality of the work, then, in the worst case, people's lives will be put at risk. But these are specific instances. As Diane Kirrane notes,[2] the *general* proposition is this: if the most important criterion for judging an action is always that it is thought to help the organisation, then certainly people outside the organisation and probably people inside it will be hurt. That's why there is huge public sympathy for whistleblowers such as Stanley Adams in his battle with pharmaceuticals giant Hoffman La Roche. What happens when an employee puts public interest, as he perceives it, above corporate loyalty? Should an organisation's pricing policies for pharmaceutical products be such as to render them unavailable to most of those who need them?

This brings us back to employees' perceptions of their organisation. If an organisation's responsibility is solely to maximise profitability for its shareholders, its main concern will be to make a profit within the law. It will only concern itself with the least it must do (the law), rather than with the best it should do (corporate ethics). Consequently, the sequence will be like this:

- *Issues* arise, often prompted by experts and whistleblowers.
- *Public opinion* becomes sensitised to them.
- The *law* prescribes certain actions relating to these issues and proscribes others.
- *Organisations* (hopefully) comply with the law.

If, however, organisations are viewed as proactive moral agents, then the sequence may be:

- *Issues* arise.
- The *organisation* formulates policies about them and takes action.
- *Public opinion* becomes activated, partly as a result of organisational actions.
- *the law* responds to public opinion.

The latter sequence transforms organisations into active moral agents who attempt to shape public opinion according to perceived ethical principles. But, of course, it assumes consent. A middle road pursues the following sequence, and is the one which most employees would probably expect:

- *Issues* arise.
- *Public opinion* becomes sensitised to them.
- *Organisations* address them.
- The *law* incorporates them.

There is some indication that organisations are addressing the issues before the law compels them to. Codes of ethics and associated structures are having much more support. Bodo Schlegelmilch and Jane Houston conducted a survey of UK organisations in 1988.[3] They sampled the 200 largest companies in the *Times* 1000, and received replies from 74. Of these, 31 had a published ethical code of practice (under whatever name). A considerable proportion of the 31 (20) had introduced the codes between 1984 and 1987. The codes recognise the inherent difficulty in making ethical decisions, but frequently came out courageously on the side of principle versus advantage. For example, Esso (UK) promises 'We will support, and we expect our managers to support, an employee who passes an opportunity or advantage which can only be secured at the sacrifice of principle.' Organisational codes of ethics in the UK tend to address the interests of a variety of stakeholders: employees, community and environment, customers, and shareholders. Few of them, however, address all these interests. Most are particularly strong in one area: Boots, for example, is concerned especially with customers: they shouldn't be misled on prices or conditions of supply, their complaints should be dealt with promptly and courteously, and after-sales service should be effective.

Unfortunately many ethical codes convey the message that this is what we, the organisation, expect of you, the employee. Not many concentrate on the rights of employees and their contract with the organisation. Yet these are the issues with which employees wearing their hats as citizens are equally concerned. Yes, they are worried if their organisation harms the environment or causes accidents. These outcomes are likely to damage their neighbours as well as themselves, and the answer to the age-old question 'Who is my neighbour?' has to be 'the human race'. But they are particularly concerned with what happens to them while they are at work. As their organisation expects more and more of them by way of corporate loyalty and service, so they expect it to act as a community. And just as the civil community seeks to ensure certain rights for its members in exchange for the obligations it imposes upon them, so, they believe, should the organisation.

As citizens, individuals are supposed to be entitled among other things to:

- defence from external attack;
- defence from internal assault;
- freedom of speech and assembly;
- due process of law;
- health and safety;
- equality of treatment regardless of gender, ethnicity, religion or sexual orientation;
- freedom of conscience;
- access to information of public concern;
- participation in a democratic process;
- freedom to improve one's lot.

They are entitled to these both as human rights and as part of a civil contract whereby they too fulfil a variety of obligations. As employees, they will come to expect nothing less than these rights (and often a great deal more as well). For example, what about freedom from predatory takeover? the opportunity to develop one's skills?

There are obvious dilemmas. For example, what about the conflict between the right to privacy and that to health and safety at work? Organisations may wish to test would-be employees for evidence of current drug abuse, since alcoholism or other forms of dependency in certain jobs may place colleagues or customers in danger. However, such testing is viewed as an infringement of civil liberties by some, despite its accepted use in the aviation, merchant shipping and oil industries.

Despite these dilemmas, people expect organisations to make an effort to guarantee that their rights are honoured. They treat such a guarantee as part of the psychological contract they have made with the organisation. And as people become more and more concerned about and aware of their rights as citizens, so they are becoming more demanding of their organisations. Yet the business trends of the 90s are pulling organisations inexorably in the opposite direction. Increased *competition*, especially cost competitiveness, can lead to cutting safety corners. It can involve industrial espionage, immoral advertising, ruthless sackings and dubious inducements. On the other hand, it *can* lead to a greater concern for safety and ethical behaviour, if and only if these are perceived to be attractive to the customer.

The *decentralisation* of decision-making means that more and more people with less and less control from the top have others' lives and well-being in their charge. The ethical codes have to be internalised, since they cannot be enforced. The opening of more markets by deregulation will mean that professional monopolies will be surrendered and professional ethics (such as they are) will no longer be valued. Globalisation opens up yet more unregulated markets, and we have already seen the unscrupulous marketing of cigarettes and pharmaceuticals in the Third World. As mergers and acquisitions increase in frequency, redundancies and the imposition of corporate cultures may ensue. And as organisations strive to adapt to and, if possible, anticipate change, they will make ever-increasing demands on their employees.

So the business environment and the social environment are apparently steaming in opposite directions at a great rate of knots. The business environment leads to greater expectations of the employee by the organisation. The social environment leads to greater ethical expectations of the organisation by the employee. These expectations appear in many cases to be mutually incompatible. And the gap is getting wider by the minute!

Professionals

But employees don't only come dressed as John or Jane Bull, citizens of the realm and of the world. They also often arrive trailing letters behind them: degrees, professional memberships, technical qualifications. While 15 per cent of UK young people currently enjoy the benefits of higher education, the percentage is far higher among our competitors, and is increasing at a phenomenal rate, especially in the Pacific rim. What expectations of organisations do professionals typically hold? The answer is of crucial importance for the 90s, given the ever-increasing dependence of organisations upon knowledge workers.

Professionals are awkward cusses from the organisation's point of view. Ask them how they earn their living, and they're almost certain to reply as engineers, scientists, accountants, lawyers, analysts. As a second thought, they may vouchsafe the information that Shell, IBM, Rank Xerox, Digital, Smith Kline Beecham or whoever actually pay their salaries. The reason is that their professional identity is a more important part of their selves than is their organisational membership. They have, after all, put a lot of effort into becoming a professional. The initiation is lengthy and painful, and often bears relatively little relationship to the professional work they're going to do later. Thereafter they are part of an exclusive group which guards entry to its ranks jealously. They are sole owners of the right to practise, and indeed perhaps this is the crucial feature which makes us uneasy if we hear hairdressers or estate agents, for example, being referred to as professionals.

Given the centrality of their profession to their personal identity, it's hardly surprising that many professionals value above all else the esteem of their professional peers. This they get for three sorts of achievement:

- pushing back the frontiers of professional knowledge;
- achieving eminence in professional practice;
- representing the profession itself by internal regulation or in external relations.

They are careful to avoid the opposite outcome – professional opprobrium – which falls upon them from a great height if they violate the professional code of ethics and are found out in this. Much in these codes refers to the fulfilment of obligations to clients and the nature of the client relationship.

So the expectations held by professionals of the organisation are entirely predictable. They want to do professional work, since they can't otherwise put their knowledge and skills to use and acquire more of them. Such development is necessary to push back the frontiers or to practise to a high level; and these are the ways in which professionals gain the esteem of their peers, which is what matters most to them. Since the organisation is a means to this end, their organisational commitment is likely to take second place to their professional commitment.

The American sociologist Alvin Gouldner spotted this potential conflict long ago, and called the typical professional a 'cosmopolitan', in contrast with the 'local' loyal Scotty types.[4]

The 1980s have seen a marked devaluation of the specialist in British organisations. Decentralisation of decision-making has meant that general managerial skills have been more in demand at ever more junior levels. Moreover, as Wendy Hirsh notes,[5] many large organisations have separated out a cohort of high fliers early in their careers, and given them rapid experience across a variety of functions. This was in order to develop a qualified resource for filling senior management positions – to ensure the succession. So in order to continue working in their professional field, employees have had to stay working in one function – research and development, production or finance for example. This has usually prevented their promotion to senior management, a signal of not being valued. The sort of 'management' they prefer is leading a team of professional colleagues and mentoring their juniors. This congenial task was available in the traditional functional department.

But the know-how organisation of the 90s isn't organised in this way. The business imperatives are the development and maintenance of core competencies, and their exploitation in the form of market-led products or services. These require quite different structures, which will be based on the competencies themselves. As we saw in chapter 3, the consequence is that technical specialists will have to collaborate with other specialists in teams. They will gain their organisational esteem from their contribution to the core competencies and their exploitation. So professional specialists will be esteemed (or not) by other specialists from *different* professions on the basis of their contribution. They will be highly valued, but not primarily by their own specialist peers.

In the long term, many professional groupings will realise that organisations rather than individuals or each other are their prime clients. When they do so, contribution to core competencies will be the basis for professional esteem and reputation. Until then, professionals and specialists may be expecting the right things (from the organisation's point of view) but for the wrong reasons. Yes, they'll have the opportunity as never before to develop their know-how. But the logic of an organisational strategy based on core competencies requires that development know-how to contribute to these competencies. Reputation in their professional community will for the present be an incidental and secondary, but valued, outcome for professional employees.

Employees

John and Jane Bull may come with or without letters after their name. But the point is – they've turned up ready for work. Workers don't need dragging to their work, nor do they require continued bribery with glossy incentives to goad them into action. What they do expect is not to have to negotiate an obstacle course before they can do what is expected of them. The employees of the next decade will demand:

- the removal of various blocks which prevent them doing their work;
- help in making transitions from job to job within the organisation;
- help in developing themselves so that they can tackle new jobs with confidence.

The *transitions* from job to job, experienced by managers in particular, are frequent and demanding. Consider, for a moment, the careers of British managers. Nigel Nicholson and Michael West looked at the nature of the job changes of over 2,000 members of the British Institute of Management in the mid-1980s.[6] They changed job on average once every three years, and more than half of these changes involved both a change of function and a change of level at the same time. Around half were moves to a newly created or newly defined job. These managers had no lengthy period of time when they were actually doing their job. So instead of the transition sequence being: preparation for the new job; encountering it and getting over the shock; adapting oneself to the job, and the job to oneself; stabilisation in the job, the last phase is often missing. There is little or no period of stability, and therefore the whole of one's working life is spent in a process of transition. So people don't so much need help with their job – they need help in making transitions and changing. No sooner have they adapted to one situation than they have to start preparing for the next.

Expectations of this sort of help will come more to the fore in the 90s. The Captain Kirks of the next decade will be making physical and cultural leaps into the unknown time after time. How do they want organisations to help them? It's not that people are desperately anxious about forthcoming job transitions. Nicholson and West's 2,000 + managers were only mildly concerned, mostly about their competence to meet the new requirements.[7] When it comes to the encounter phase there's more dissatisfaction – the organisation is held to blame for its constricting practices. There's likely to be more stress when the person's fit with the new environment is bad; when they can't predict what the job's going to involve; and when they feel they have little personal control over it. Overall, though, job transitions don't cause negative outcomes, but positive ones: people who have changed jobs have feelings of challenge, freedom, authority, satisfaction and fulfilment. Many of them 'hit the ground running', adapting the job to their own preferences and strengths.

What individuals *do* expect from organisations are the appropriate support systems to ease the transition process. Traditionally recommended systems are career counselling and recruitment/transfer procedures for the preparation stage; induction and socialisation for encounter; job design, training and supervision for adjustment; and information and management systems of control for stabilisation. But, as we shall see, these systems are often not designed to be of much use. They are not embedded in a culture which trusts individuals to do their jobs and enables them by providing the opportunities for them to do so. Instead the attitude is often one of 'in at the deep end, never did me any harm'. Above all, most organisations appear to see most job transitions as serving their own immediate needs rather than as developing individuals for the longer term. To quote the dismal conclusions of Nicholson and West, 'Our own research has painted a bleak picture of organisational involvement (or rather the lack of it), in career development. It seems that most companies act as if their responsibility for managing transitions begins and ends with recruitment procedures.'[8] As these authors note, huge and unexpected changes in structure happen more and more often in organisations these days. Layers of management are stripped out, or mergers result in a radical restructure. So it will be of no use leaving the organisational structure and hierarchy to provide career opportunities for people; they can't rely on them being there much longer. Employees will expect more help in the 90s.

They will have another very reasonable expectation as well – this, too, in response to the organisation's expectations of them. If they are going to keep up to date, be innovative, move into newly created jobs, take more responsibility and get close to the customer they are going to have to develop themselves as never before. Hitherto uncreated jobs can't be trained for; employees have to develop themselves so as to be capable of taking them on at short notice. Employees will expect organisations to give them the opportunity to develop.

Self-development is an ambiguous phrase – does it mean development *of* the self or *by* the self or both of these? Some organisations are putting the onus on individuals to take responsibility for their own development, but at the same time making it next to impossible for them to do so by

- allocation to jobs for short-term reasons only;
- lack of opportunity for out-of-work learning;
- absence of any co-ordination of job allocation, outside learning, secondments and so on into an individual development strategy.

During the next decade, employees will accept neither the Scylla of non-developmental job placement nor the Charybdis of unsupported responsibility for self-development. They will expect mutually agreed support.

Individuals

But above all, people come to work as themselves. They bring all their individual differences with them, especially their differences in values. Organisations will utterly fail to understand employees' expectations unless they realise that:

- employees have different value priorities from each other, though there will be groups whose values are similar;
- they often have different value priorities at different stages of their careers and their lives;
- those with the power in organisations are likely to misperceive the value priorities of others;
- value priorities have changed in general over the past few years and are likely to continue to do so.

Throughout the history of our thinking about people at work we've desperately sought the key to their motivation; as though they need to be goaded from the rear or given the incentive of a carrot dangled a short way in front of their noses. What would the magic carrot be? Money, the universal pre-war remedy? Or the esteem of colleagues and management, the philosopher's stone of the human relations movement of the 50s? Or the more sophisticated schemes of Herzberg and Maslow, still the staple offerings of many courses in management? These gurus imply that once management has ensured the meeting of more 'basic' needs, more 'advanced' ones come into play, such as autonomy or self-actualisation. In effect, therefore, the management theorists of the past have sought to show that everyone was motivated by a particular need or value; the more recent of them adding the rider, 'provided various other needs have been met'. All these theorists downplayed the range of individual differences; perhaps they did so because their underlying purpose was to help organisations devise systems which treated employees alike. You can design work or reward systems which apply across the board only if you assume that people want the same things out of work.

Various theorists have recognised that these assumptions aren't tenable. Victor Vroom for example, refused to consider motivation as dependent on any particular reward *content* at all.[9] He saw it as a *process*, in which people put in effort to the extent that they thought it would enable them to do various things; that these actions would have various outcomes; and that they valued those outcomes. So a salesperson might put in a lot of hours on the road because she believes this would increase her client base; she believes that more clients would increase her sales; and that an increase in sales would lead to her promotion to sales manager. This she values because it will enable her to spend more time at home. Of course, she may be mistaken in her beliefs – more clients may not lead to more sales, which might actually be improved if she cultivated her existing bigger clients more. And her values may change – home life might not be such a pull as her children get older. But it is what *she* believes will happen and what *she* values that will motivate her.

More in line with our concentration on career, Ed Schein has enumerated several 'career anchors'.[10] These are defined as patterns of self-perceived talents, motives and values that serve to guide, constrain, stabilise and integrate individual careers. Schein derived five such anchors from his long-term study of MBA graduates from the Massachusetts Institute of Technology. The first was *technical/functional competence*. Individuals who had this as their primary anchor wanted to remain challenged in their area of expertise. Those favouring *managerial competence* valued exercising responsibility and linking organisational achievements to their own efforts. *Security and stability* followers valued continuity in employment, in neighbourhood and in family. The group who valued *creativity* organised all their career decisions around the need to create something: a product, a service or a company of their own, perhaps even a monument to their working life. Finally, individuals with the anchor of *autonomy and independence* valued autonomous careers such as consultancy, and found large organisations most uncongenial. Schein's anchors are derived from a sample of highly educated Americans; we might expect to find other anchors in different types of employee. But the point to be made here is that even within such a homogeneous group, individuals differed at a fundamental level. The extent to which people are explicitly aware of their anchor, and of other possible anchors, is unclear, but we can be pretty sure that in any organisation most if not all of the anchors are to be found. Quite often a high proportion of people in a particular department may have the same anchor. Many people in research and development, for example, are likely to have technical/functional competence as their anchor.

So individual employees are likely to differ from each other as to which career anchor is paramount for them. They will expect different things from their organisation, because they want different things out of their work. And these differences will increase during the next decade. For the flip side of internationalisation of business is the internationalisation of employment. Global organisations will be employing staff all over the world. Nationally based organisations in the UK will be recruiting from abroad as employment restrictions are relaxed in 1992. So all of the differences in underlying values and assumptions which Captain Kirk is expected to explore will actually return with him to home base. Employees will come from cultures in which relationships at work are valued highly, or where a sense of order and predictability pervade the organisation. While allowing for individual differences, it is likely that in general, people from, say, Japan will be more likely to have the anchor of security and stability as their priority than people from the USA.

There is some evidence that this is so. C. Brooklyn Derr and André Laurent conducted a study of 84 French, German, British and Swedish managers of a large multinational organisation.[11] They found that the French held much more strongly than the others to the career orientation of 'getting balanced' (finding an equilibrium between personal and professional life, and akin to Schein's anchor of security and stability). In terms of 'getting high' (being excited by the work itself, and related to Schein's creativity and technical/functional anchors), the order from the top was Swedes, French, British and Germans.

Not only do people differ from each other in their work values, they also change during the course of their lives. Specific events, such as divorce or redundancy, may underly such value changes; or the taking up and relinquishing of different roles, as suggested by Donald Super's life-career rainbow.[12] Super proposes that certain roles are apt to come upon us at certain particular periods of our lives. These roles are the bands of the rainbow, which shine more strongly at particular periods in one's life. He argues that such responsibilities as those of spouse and parent, and of child of ageing parents, will change our value priorities and self-concept.

Obviously, the career anchor of security and stability may come more to the fore at such periods. Indeed, Fran and Charles Rodgers found that up to 35 per cent of working men and women in the USA with young children have told their bosses they will not take jobs involving shift work, relocation, extensive travel, intense pressure or lots of overtime.[13] Since these jobs are often offers of promotion, they are taking a specific career option which reflects an anchor of security and stability rather than, say, managerial competence.

Apart from such life events as parenthood, however, it's likely that careers in general can be characterised as going through various stages. Michael Arthur and Kathy Kram suggest three stages, claiming that their theory reflects the theory and research of many others.[14] Their stages are exploring, directedness and protecting. *Exploring* may last to the early to mid-30s. In this stage, the individual develops his or her competence at the job, and forms an occupational identity. They learn a lot by doing, especially by performing technical or functional tasks, and often demonstrate energy and exuberance. During the middle career period, that of *directedness*, individuals have become clear about some career anchors. The career anchor of managerial competence may well gain preference over technical and functional competence for many people at this stage. After mid to late 40s, people enter the *protecting* stage. They need to secure and maintain their status, experience continued affirmation of their work, and pass on the benefits of their learning and experience to others. Each of these three stages builds on the other rather than replacing it. So the individuals in the third stage are stewards of what they have acquired over their careers. Perhaps, though, we need to be a bit more cautious about relating ages to stages. Some older people may pass much more rapidly through all these stages.

One of the major demographic trends of the 90s will be the increased employment or return to employment of older people. These employees will expect their knowledge and experience to be put to good use; they want to help maintain the organisation. Given that organisational survival requires a balance between adaptation to the environment and maintenance, they should be able to play a crucial role; they will certainly expect to do so. What's more, many of them will be financially self-sufficient, having inherited property from their parents – they will be able to pick and choose, and will expect their employment to fit in with their leisure pursuits.

But the biggest area of recruitment during the 1990s in the UK will not be of people from different cultures, nor of older workers;

it will be of *women*. Various estimates put the proportion of the new jobs of the 90s that will be filled by women at between 70 and 80 per cent. And just as we can discern different career anchors as typical of those groups, so there is now overwhelming evidence that women typically have different career anchors from men.

According to Joan Gallos,[15] women's key concern is how 'to manage life's critical adult challenge – the balance between love and work'. This means they are more likely to be concerned with Derr's getting balanced than with getting ahead (upward mobility), getting secure (company loyalty and a sense of belonging), or getting free (autonomy). They value interdependence more than independence. They see their career accomplishments not only as individual achievements but in the context of supportive relationships. Much of the theorising about career development is based on research into samples of men; as a consequence, men are only now realising that the stages in women's careers may be entirely different at present from those of men. Whereas men in general move from individual development through to concern for maintenance and the mentoring of junior colleagues, women in general go in the opposite direction. They start with connections with others, manage to become separate, and finally see themselves as individually equal to others. Note, though, the caveat 'in general' – there are many reasons for different careers other than gender.

Clearly, those organisational cultures which stress individuality and the power to get things done, the hero standing on his own two feet and going it alone, are inimical to women's developmental career anchors. Indeed, research by Virginia Schein found that adjectives used to describe 'the successful middle manager' (assertive, ambitious, and so on) were almost identical to those used to describe men, and diametrically opposed to those describing women.[16] On the contrary, women are going to expect organisations to allow them to exercise their talents for forming and sustaining relationships. This is *not* synonymous with being subservient to and dependent on one's superiors; it is entirely in accord with an increased emphasis in the 90s on working together on project teams. The organisation will *need* people who define themselves interpersonally as well as personally. It will need networking more than hierarchy, mutual collaboration more than competition. The key issue is – will it want such people? The question is no sooner raised than answered – it's going to have them anyway. So if it is going to benefit from them, it had better offer them two things at least: the opportunity to express their values and talents, and the working arrangements they want to fit in with their other commitments. In dual-career families, mobility will be an issue. A recent CBI survey showed that half of the organisations surveyed could not persuade employees to relocate because of clashes with their partner's career.[17]

The impact of women will be immense if organisations do adapt to their increasing presence. For in addition to their career emphasis on forming and sustaining relationships, managerial women differ from men in other respects. Returning to Nicholson and West's sample of UK managers, female managers of the mid-80s were more highly educated and occupied more specialist positions than their male counterparts.[18] They had higher needs for personal growth, and were more motivated by the intrinsic features of the job itself. They were less materialistic and concerned with status than their male colleagues. Organisations' need for knowledge workers and their continued development seems matched by an underutilised source of such labour – women.

So internationalisation and demographic changes of the 90s mean that more people from other cultures, more older workers and more women will be employees. Each will bring their own typical values and career anchors, which is not to deny that each one is an individual but to affirm that with their employment the probability that certain values and expectations will become more prominent is increased. However, there is yet another source of changed expectations: general *societal changes* in values and attitudes.

The most reliable evidence of these changes is to be found in the surveys conducted by Social and Community Planning Research over the past few years.[19] Their research on social attitudes in the UK demonstrates some clear trends which we may suppose will continue in the same direction during the 90s. Here are some of the more relevant ones for organisations: the figures are for 1989, with responses to the same question posed in 1983 in brackets. Concerning women and work, 69 per cent of women (33) disagreed with the statement 'The wife's job is to look after the home and family', and 61 percent (34) with 'A job is all right but what women really want is home and children.' The percentages for men were somewhat, but not markedly, lower. Concerning the environment, 75 per cent of all respondents (62) thought that industrial waste in rivers or sea was a 'very serious' environmental hazard. The statement that 'Industry should be prevented from causing damage to the countryside, even if this sometimes leads to higher prices' was agreed by 88 per cent (78 in 1983). So two of the social changes we have discussed are supported by a sound nationwide sample. Again, we have to assume that employees will bring these changed attitudes and values to work with them; and they will expect organisations to act accordingly – unless of course, their jobs are threatened!

Before I sum up this chapter I need to sound a note of warning about my analysis. Throughout this book I have talked in rather simplistic terms of 'the organisation' and 'the individual' dealing with each other. Indeed, in this chapter I have stressed that organisations *are* perceived as moral agents, accountable for their actions. However, Dian Hosking and Stephen Fineman have recently reminded us that the members of organisations actively seek to influence other members to create the organisational value system.[20] Individuals join with others sharing the same value priorities to form interest groups, and some interest groups are more powerful than others. So individuals aren't on their own when they seek the fulfilment of their expectations – others are with them.

Particularly when there is a great deal of change and ambiguity, existing interests are threatened and influence attempts become highly political. Thus power becomes more important, and it is in the hands of the most powerful whether the expectations of other less powerful groups are met. The most powerful grouping is often of those who are in senior management positions. This is the paradox of change: those whose values and interests have most influence over the organisation gain yet more power when change becomes overwhelming. Yet it is precisely their values which need to change, since it is they who tend to be proxy for 'the organisation'.

We have considered in this chapter the expectations of individuals: as citizens and consumers, as professionals, as workers, and as themselves. They hold these expectations of the organisation, *of which they are themselves part*. The extent to which their expectations are met reflects their power in the organisation, as individuals and as members of interest groups. But if the 'business imperatives' are as I described them in chapter 2, and if their implications for employment are correctly inferred in chapter 3, the gap between what most people seem to want from their career and what will be expected of them seems at first sight a huge one to jump. In the next chapter we eye up the distance and discuss whether it is jumpable.

Some final questions

About your own career
- What do you believe should be your rights as an employee?

- Which of them do you currently enjoy?
- Is this situation likely to change, and if so, how?
- Would you categorise yourself as a professional? If so, to whom do you owe the greater commitment: your profession or your organisation? What implications does your answer have for your career?
- Have you recently changed jobs within your organisation? What went right in the actual transition? What went wrong?
- Read again the description of career anchors. Which is your prime career anchor? What implications does this have for your career?
- What stage of your career are you in – exploring, directedness or protecting? Does your present job suit the stage you're at? If not, why not? What sort of job *would* fit?
- Do you have a spouse or partner? Does he or she have an organisational career? What difference has the existence of two careers had upon your own?

About the organisation

- Does your organisation ever anticipate legal requirements? In which areas of practice?
- Think of an ethical dilemma your organisation faces. On what basis does it solve it?
- Does your organisation have a published code of ethics? What effect does it have in practice?
- What help does your organisation give in managing job transitions?
- What are the underlying assumptions in your organisational culture about why people work? How do these assumptions affect their reward and career systems?
- How does your organisation support the careers of women? Of older returners?

Notes

1 M. Friedman (1970) 'The social responsibility of business is to increase profits', *New York Times Magazine*, 13 September: 32.

2 D. Kirrane (1990) 'Managing values: a systematic approach to business ethics', *Training and Development Journal*, November: 53–66.

3 B.B. Schlegelmilch and J.E. Houston (1990) 'Corporate codes of ethics', *Management Decision*, 28 (7): 38–43.

4 A.W. Gouldner (1957) 'Cosmopolitans and locals: towards an analysis of latent social roles', *Administrative Science Quarterly*, 2: 282–92.

5 W. Hirsh (1990) *Succession Planning: Correct Practice and Future Issues*. Brighton: Institute of Manpower Studies.

6 N. Nicholson and M. West (1988) *Managerial Job Change: Men and Women in Transition*. Cambridge: Cambridge University Press.

7 N. Nicholson and M. West (1989) 'Transitions, work histories, and careers', in M.B. Arthur, D.T. Hall and B.S. Lawrence (eds), *Handbook of Career Theory*. Cambridge: Cambridge University Press.

8 Ibid., p. 193.

9 V.H. Vroom (1964) *Work and Motivation*. New York: Wiley.

10 E.H. Schein (1978) *Career Dynamics: Matching Individual and Organisational Needs*. Reading, Massachusetts: Addison-Wesley.

11 C.B. Derr and A. Laurent (1989) 'The internal and external career: a theoretical and cross-cultural perspective', in M.B. Arthur, D.T. Hall and B.S. Lawrence (eds), *Handbook of Career Theory*. Cambridge: Cambridge University Press.

12 D.E. Super (1980) 'A life-span life-space approach to career development', *Journal of Vocational Behaviour*, 26: 282–98.

13 F.S. Rodgers and C. Rodgers (1989) 'Business and the facts of family life', *Harvard Business Review*, 89 (6): 121–9.

14 M.B. Arthur and K.E. Kram (1989) 'Reciprocity at work: the separate, yet inseparable possibilities for individual and organisational development', in M.B. Arthur, D.T. Hall and B.S. Lawrence (eds), *Handbook of Career Theory*. Cambridge: Cambridge University Press.

15 J.V. Gallos (1989) 'Exploring women's development: implications for career theory, practice, and research', in M.B. Arthur, D.T. Hall and B.S. Lawrence (eds), *Handbook of Career Theory*. Cambridge: Cambridge University Press.

16 V.E. Schein (1973) 'The relationship between sex role stereotypes and requisite management characteristics', *Journal of Applied Psychology*, 57: 95–100.

17 Confederation of British Industry (1990) *Spouses, Partners, and Domestic Assignments*. London: CBI.

18 Nicholson and West (1988), op. cit.

19 R. Jowell, S. Witherspoon and L. Brook (1990) *British Social Attitudes: The 7th Report*. London: Gower Press.

20 D. Hosking and S. Fineman (1990) 'Organising processes', *Journal of Management Studies*, 27 (6): 583–604.

5

Balancing Acts

Organisation and individual

Four themes underlying organisations' expectations were outlined in chapter 3. Ideal employees of the 90s are going to welcome *adventure and exploration*. They are going to be *loyal and committed* to the organisation. They are going to *communicate* their expert knowledge to others and *collaborate* with them. And they are going to make *intelligent sense* of their environment in the light of business strategy.

Employees' expectations as reviewed in chapter 4 didn't always seem to chime in with those of the organisation. Some parallel but countervailing themes emerged. Yes, they were certainly not averse to adventure and exploration but they wanted *support* from home base. Loyalty and commitment to the organisation were all very well, but they insisted that the organisation recognise that they too had *rights and needs* as individuals and as members of interest groups. They could only identify with the organisation if it was congruent with their personal identity. Communication of their professional knowledge and collaboration with others in the organisation is essential, they felt, but where will the *recognition* come from which they've traditionally got from their professional peers? Are they going to be valued for their expertise? And it is all very stimulating to be the organisation's eyes and ears at the interface with the customer and the competitor, but will they have the *autonomy* to react innovatively? Or won't they be trusted to do so? And will the organisation pay any attention to what they tell it about the customer?

The key human resource task in the 90s is to reconcile these two sets of expectations – the organisation's and the individual's. Surviving organisations will be those which achieve all of the following balancing acts:

- adventure and exploration, together with proper support;
- loyalty and commitment, together with respect for individuality;
- knowledge and its communication, together with tolerance and recognition;

– environmental intelligence, together with trust and autonomy.

Organisations have to find ways of adequately responding to the needs of those from whom they expect so much: needs for support, respect, tolerance, and trust. Strategies will be successful only if they achieve all of these four balances. The task of achieving each balance, however, is dwarfed by that of ensuring that all four balances are compatible with each other. *Starship Enterprise* is doomed if Kirk's support system and Spock's scientific licence make Scotty mutinous and send Uhura to sleep.

The great temptation at this point is to try to devise a set of human resource systems which achieve all four balances satisfactorily. The technological fix beckons seductively. We could boast of having 'constructed some strategic architecture' for human resources. Or, to get back to the metaphor which still dominates so much of our thinking about organisations, we could say we'd established some smoothly working parts to the organisational machine. But systems are artifacts. Even when they work well, they are merely expressions of underlying values and assumptions. If they make no sense to their users, they are ignored, subverted or dealt with as cursorily as possible. The first task, therefore, is to discover what values and assumptions might result in the achievement of our four balancing tricks. What might be an appropriate human resource culture for the 90s? Only when we have these basic features of culture clear can we start thinking about the artifacts which express them. The dangers of the reverse sequence are only too clear. If we go straight for the systems, we will finish up with structures that suit the organisation. They offer administrative tidiness and efficiency; but they treat people *en masse*, ignoring their individuality. And the one thing which stands out from our analysis so far is that unilateral decision-making by those in positions of power in organisations will have to give way to psychological contracting with other individual employees.

So what are the four balancing acts likely to look like? What delicate combinations of values and assumptions will underpin them? The first balancing act is that of Captain Kirk, venturing out into the uncertain cultural void, with the safety-net underneath (*Starship Enterprise* is now a circus act!). How do we reconcile the organisation's expectations of personal change and adventure into new territories with the individual's expectations for support? Support in the exploratory journey itself, the transitions from place to place; support in the personal development which fits them for the journey; and support in their other roles besides the work role.

What are the key values and assumptions which underpin a successful balancing act?

In terms of values, I propose that a high value should be placed on:

- responsiveness to change;
- risk and innovation;
- tolerance of failures;
- development of people;
- supportive teamwork.

Among the key underlying assumptions are that:

- people can change;
- people can like change;
- people need help;
- people help each other;
- organisation is there to support people.

The second balancing act is that between the organisation's expectations of loyalty and commitment, and people's need to be treated as individuals with rights of their own. Some of the key values here are that a high priority should be placed on:

- honouring agreements;
- mutual loyalty (rather than loyalty to the more powerful);
- respecting rights;
- deserving rewards (not granting favours);
- respecting individuality;
- making agreements explicit;
- experience and organisational knowledge.

Among the underpinning assumptions are that:

- people can respect agreements;
- people can trust each other;
- people have rights;
- people want different things;
- people have individual identities;
- people like to know where they stand;
- people make sense of their organisation.

Our third balancing trick is to reconcile the organisation's need to use its experts to boost its core competencies with those experts' own needs for licence and to be valued. How can one honour the professional culture that values individual expertise while meeting the organisational need to cultivate core competencies across professional groupings?

Highly valued will be:

- knowledge of the core competencies;
- the star specialists who drive them;
- communication and collaboration.

Among the key assumptions are that:

- organisations survive by know-how;
- some people are motivated to be expert;
- different experts can collaborate.

Finally, how can we achieve synergy between the organisation's needs to adapt to local markets and to gain knowledge about developments in its environment, and individuals' needs for autonomy and trust in their own local market segment?

The culture will have to place a high value on:

- local knowledge;
- boundary people who interface with customers and predict their needs;
- communication of strategy;
- innovative local initiatives.

It will have to assume that:

- people can discover their customers' needs;
- people can inform others of those needs;
- people can understand and work to a strategic vision;
- people can help formulate one.

Four separate cultural balancing acts have been rashly attempted so far. But the most difficult task of all remains: how can we balance the balancing acts? Many suggestions have been made recently about individual balancing acts. In particular, top billing has been granted to Captain Kirk and Mr Spock. We've had accounts of how organisations should develop managers to become adaptable international business people;[1] and we've had helpful blueprints for optimising organisations' utilisation of their experts.[2] But Scotty and Uhura have tended to miss out. We hear relatively little about individuals' rights (but quite a lot about their organisational commitment). And while grand designs for corporate strategy emanate from the centre, the boundary workers' knowledge of their environment which should inform strategy is seldom stressed.

But more important, these four balancing acts are rarely attempted together. If our analysis of the business and social environment of the 90s is reasonably accurate, then *all four* themes will dominate organisational thinking. All four balancing acts will have to be achieved simultaneously if organisations are to survive even the predictable trends. As for wars and rumours of wars —. So where are the contradictions in the culture? Where are the conflicting pressures which threaten the overall balance? As we reread our lists of values and assumptions, some dilemmas become painfully obvious:

- We're valuing change and development, but we're also valuing steady loyalty and organisational experience.
- We're encouraging individual stars, but also cross-functional collaboration.
- We're valuing local initiatives, but also nurturing core organisation-wide competencies.
- We're concerned with individually based rewards and careers, but we value collaborative teamwork.

In sum, it is the two age-old dilemmas rearing their hoary heads again: first, how to reconcile the individual and the collective interest; and secondly, how to maintain an organisation in existence while it changes to adapt to its environment.

For Ed Schein the main purpose of an organisational culture is to form a bridge between the past and the future.[3] The culture embodies the values and assumptions which have brought it to its present state of development. Yet it permits change and adaption because its values and assumptions move with the times. What sort of culture will permit the four sets of values and assumptions to coexist? Such coexistence is likely to be necessary for survival in the 90s. My answer is that the sort of culture required is one with certain overarching values; these make it possible to hold conflicting values simultaneously in tension within the organisation. One such overarching value is that of *diversity of values*. It will be recognised that many specialists will always value technical know-how higher than anything else, for example. The point is that they should also value collaboration in the development of the core competence. The survivors' culture of the 90s will be one which actively values diverse value priorities. It will recognise that it is good that its Kirks put the highest premium on development; that its Spocks value their expertise above all else; that the Scotties keep going because they need to be needed; and that many of its employees, like Uhura, simply want the opportunity to use their local knowledge to do their job in their own neck of the woods. For only a culture which puts a positive value upon value diversity will retain the loyalty of such a diverse crew; and it needs them all for its survival.

There is a second overarching value for the 90s culture: a value which justifies the use of the word 'career' in the title of this book. It is giving the highest priority to the *psychological contract*. It is only when individuals and organisations negotiate and renegotiate their psychological contract that their relationship can last. For as their environment changes, so do the expectations of both parties. To keep them in balance is a continuous task, and only an organisation which actively seeks to reconcile its employees' needs with its own will survive. So the idea of the organisational career is central; on this analysis, *the career is the sequence of psychological contracts which binds the parties together.*

These two meta-values – value diversity and psychological contracting – are the conditions for change. Successful change requires a balance of people and their continued mutual trust and commitment. Any organisational culture which neglects these overarching values will be in danger of failing; failing in its function of adapting the learning of the past to the needs of the future.

Current realities

But enough of prescriptions disguised as prophecies. What is the current state of the psychological contract? How far is the reality from the perfect balancing act I've just described?

The psychological contract implies reciprocity. It implies that organisation and individual take each other's point of view into account. But some other preconditions also have to be met before a successful contract can be concluded. The first is obvious. There has to be some point of contact, some degree of overlap, between what each party wants and what they think the other wants. If I want to develop my technical expertise but I believe my organisation wants me to become a generalist manager, there's little overlap as far as I'm concerned. Or look at it from the organisation's point of view. If they want me to do a stint in Italy but think that I'll be unwilling for family reasons there is little point of contact there for them either.

This first precondition makes the basic point that each party to a contract acts on the basis of what they *believe* the other's position to be. But they may be mistaken. My organisation may actually value my expertise more than my potential as a general manager. I may in fact be willing to commute to Italy weekly. So another precondition is that each party has a tolerably accurate picture of what the other wants. Mistaken perceptions can result in contracts which are bound to fall through as soon as the reality becomes clear. Then the real differences can be explored.

The organisation and the individual can focus on what each

really does want, and start negotiating and compromising towards an agreement. But if the gap remains too wide then a satisfactory contract can't be made. Each party may withdraw, psychologically or physically. Employees may work to their job descriptions; organisations may give them non-jobs. Or employees may leave for other employment or be 'encouraged' to do so by their organisation.

How far are these preconditions met in practice? How big are the gaps between what people want and what they think their organisation wants (and vice versa)? How accurate are they in their perceptions of the other? And when all the misperceptions are removed, what are the real gaps which still have to be bridged?

These were the questions Carole Pemberton, Rob Pinder and I asked in our most recent piece of research.[4] We approached four large UK-based organisations: a bank, a retail organisation, a hi-tech manufacturer and a security firm. We asked a sample of their managers, together with *their* bosses, to complete a questionnaire. We received 139 responses from managers from all four organisations, but only the first three felt able to ask bosses to join in as well. So we had 98 pairs of managers and their bosses from three different sectors.

We asked about a whole variety of career topics: long-term objectives; Ed Schein's career anchors;[5] how job moves are managed; intentions to leave; and various personal and career history details. Three factors emerged from analysis of the responses:

- 'Anchors', which contained questions about challenge, skills, information, networks, power, independence and achievement;
- 'Promotion', which consisted of two questions:
  'How much would you want ultimately to reach senior management status?'
  'How much would you want to have reached the highest position you are going to reach within five years?'
- 'Development' – two questions again:
  'How much would you want your next job to require a major increase in your general managerial competence?'
  'In your professional or technical competence?'

But it wasn't the questions we asked which were novel – it was how we asked them. The same questions were asked three times of each manager in three different ways, and three times of their bosses. For *managers*, the instructions before the three sets of questions were as follows:

- This part of the career audit asks you about what you believe will happen. How likely is it that . . .
- The next part of the audit asks you what you would ideally like to happen. How much would you want . . .
- The next part asks you what you think others in your organisation who have an important influence on your career would like to happen. How much would they want . . .

For their *bosses*, the instructions ran like this:

- This part of the career audit asks you what you believe will happen with reference to the career of Jane Bloggs. How likely is it that . . .
- This part of the audit asks you what you would ideally like to happen in the career of Jane Bloggs. How much would you want her to . . .
- The next part of the audit asks you what you think Jane Bloggs would like to happen. How much would she want . . .

So both parties were asked what they thought would happen regarding the manager's career, what they would like to happen, and what they thought the other wanted to happen.

The first research question we asked was where these three factors – anchors, promotion and development – came from in the first place. What predicts how strongly people will feel about them? The answer was clear-cut: when all the personal factors, such as age and gender, and all the career variables, such as average length of time in a job, were put into the equation, one emerged as the major predictor. It was the length of service in the organisation. The longer people had been with the organisation, the less likely they believed themselves to achieve anchors or development, and the less they valued them.

Promotion follows a different pattern. The managers thought they were more likely to be promoted if they'd spent less time on average in each job. And they wanted promotion more the more often they'd been promoted in the past and the shorter the length of their immediately previous job.

So managers' aspirations for and expectations of general rewards and development fade the longer they stay; cynicism – or is it realism? – sets in. But it's different with promotion. If they've been moved around a lot, they think they'll be promoted – the crown prince syndrome of the fast trackers described by Wendy Hirsh.[6] And the more promotion managers get, the more they want – some people are never satisfied.

So much for the origins of our managers' feelings about their careers. The results suggest that their relationships with their organisations are the key predictor. What we were really interested in, though, was the psychological contract. To what extent are the preconditions for the contract met in British industry and commerce today?

First we looked at the degree of difference between what each party wanted and what they thought the other wanted. This, after all, is the basis for their initial approach to making a career contract. Figure 5.1 shows the picture for the managers, and Figure 5.2 for the bosses. A rating of 2 indicates 'definitely want', 1 'would like', 0 'does not matter', −1 'would not like', −2 'definitely do not want'. So overall, managers believe that their bosses want significantly less favourable career outcomes for them than they want for themselves. Bosses, on the other hand, believe that their subordinates want significantly more anchors and development than they want to give them; not the ideal way to approach a negotiation. Promotion is the biggest area of contention. For while bosses recognise that subordinates are likely to want more anchors and development than they want to give, they don't have the same perception of promotion.

But how accurate are these perceptions anyway? What happens when we compare what bosses believe that managers want with what they actually do want (Fig. 5.3)? And conversely, what

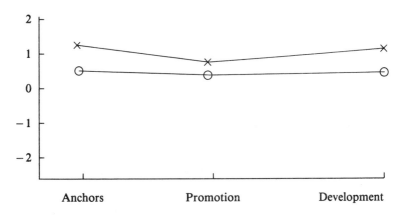

× managers' preferences
o managers' perceptions of bosses' preferences

Figure 5.1 *Managers' preferences versus their perceptions of bosses' preferences*

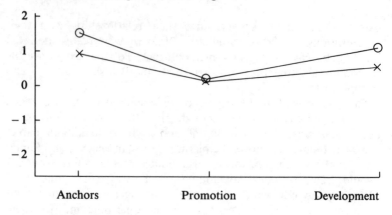

× bosses' preferences
o bosses' perceptions of managers' preferences

Figure 5.2   *Bosses' preferences versus their perceptions of managers' preferences*

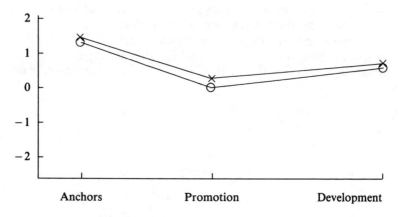

× managers' preferences
o bosses' perceptions of managers' preferences

Figure 5.3   *Managers' preferences versus bosses' perceptions of those preferences*

managers believe that bosses want with the reality of *their* preferences (Fig 5.4)?

There are a couple of areas where misunderstanding is rife:

– Bosses underestimate managers' aspirations for promotion.
– Managers underestimate their bosses' concern that their anchors should be strengthened.

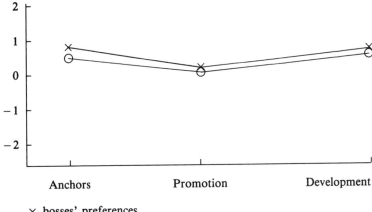

x bosses' preferences
o managers' perceptions of bosses' preferences

Figure 5.4 *Bosses' preferences versus managers' perceptions of those preferences*

But these differences are differences between the overall averages of each group of 98. They simply indicate to what extent each group as a whole over- or underestimates the other group's aspirations. What we are really interested in is each of the 98 pairs; the individual manager, each with his or her boss. How accurate are these individual perceptions? The way to look at this issue is to compute correlation coefficients. While perceptions may not be entirely accurate, at least we would expect a relatively high estimate of a high aspiration, and a lower estimate of a low one. There should be some degree of synch between the members of each pair. Results indicated that there were no statistically significant correlations at all. The parties were largely in the dark about what each other wanted, although they thought they knew.

But let's suppose that they weren't. Let's suppose that each accurately perceived what the other wanted. Then they would be able to compare what each really wanted with what the other really wanted. Figure 5.5 provides this comparison, while Figure 5.6 shows the differences between their beliefs about what the outcomes will be. Apart from managers believing that they are slightly more likely to be promoted than their bosses believe them to be, both have an equally reasonably optimistic view of the future, at least with respect to anchors and promotion (a rating of 0.4 indicates a belief that an outcome is fairly unlikely, one of 0.6 that it is fairly likely). But the major differences occur in preferences. As Figure 5.5 demonstrates, managers have much

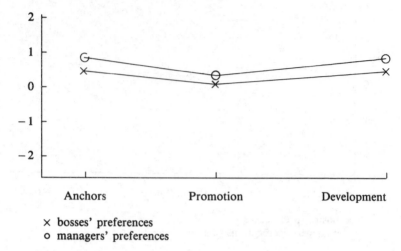

Figure 5.5   *Bosses' preferences versus managers' preferences*

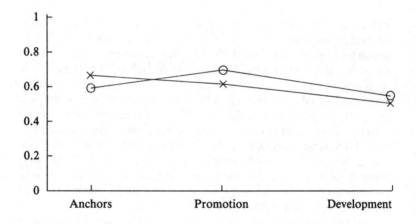

Figure 5.6   *Bosses' versus managers' beliefs about outcome probabilities*

higher aspirations for all three factors than their bosses have for them; and very low correlations indicate minimal individual agreement. So managers' cynicism was justified (Figure 5.1); they do want more for themselves than their bosses are prepared to give. A classic start to a negotiation, we're tempted to say. But when there's so much confusion and misperception at the individual level, it doesn't augur well for fruitful compromise.

We haven't yet asked the most basic question of all, though. Do these managers actually think of their careers as appropriate topics for negotiation? If they do, then both their own wishes *and* their perceptions of what their organisation would like should affect their career decisions. In order to discover whether this was actually happening, we looked at managers' intentions to leave the organisation. We asked them two questions:

- How likely is it that you will choose to leave the organisation within the next three years?
- How likely is it that you would accept the first offer of a preferable job that you receive from another organisation?

Intentions to leave, we felt, were a good index of the state of health of the psychological contract. After all, what is more indicative of the deteriorating state of a relationship than the intention to quit it for ever? We put the measures of the managers' attitudes towards anchors, promotion and development into a predictive equation, together with two other possible predictors: their perceptions of their bosses' preferences for them on the three factors; and their perception of the state of the labour market. This last we assessed by the question:

- How likely is it that you could find a preferable job with another organisation within six months?

The results were fascinating. As we predicted from the previous research literature, perception of the labour market was the most powerful predictor. But the next was more surprising: it was managers' perceptions of their bosses' preferences regarding their promotion. If managers believed that their bosses didn't favour their promotion, then they were willing to quit.

This result says two things very powerfully. The first is that despite all the current talk of the power of management development as a reward and a motivator, what actually prompts action is promotion prospects. And secondly, as far as managers are concerned, there is little sign of a psychological contract operating anyway. Promotion prospects predict intention to leave, and these prospects are seen as being entirely at the disposition of one's organisation.

To check on this interpretation, we divided our managers into two subgroups. The first, and far larger, group believed that the decision on their next job rested more with others than with themselves; the second the reverse. For the majority group, labour

market and perception of bosses' wishes continued to predict intention to leave. For the second group, they didn't. So we can
conclude that perceived bosses' wishes predict intention to leave
only for those who think that careers are a matter for the organisation to dispose as it wishes.

This is a depressing picture. If we generalise from career moves
to the four balances described at the beginning of this chapter, they
certainly seem pie in the sky compared to the reality. But one single
finding in the research literature does strike a more optimistic note.
Denise Rousseau questioned 224 US MBA students who had
recently accepted job offers.[7] They pictured themselves as about
to enter a psychological contract where their hard work and willingness to take on extra tasks would be rewarded by high and
performance-based pay, and training and development; and where
their willingness to stay longer than a minimum length of time with
their employer would be recompensed by a degree of job security.
Fond hopes from those wet behind the ears, our hard-bitten sample
of 40-year-olds would reply!

So the current state of the psychological contract seems
miserable, according to our admittedly limited sample. Why is the
gap between ideal and reality so wide that it might better be
described as a yawning chasm?

Chapter 6 will try to come up with some answers. I will argue
that some organisations have a steady business strategy and a
human resource policy to match. In these organisations at least one
or two of our four balances will be met. Others, though, are in the
midst of the profound business changes of the present decade (see
chapter 2). For these, the balances they had successfully struck
have been lost. Their headlong rush into the business future has
shattered whatever psychological contracts they had with their
shell-shocked employees.

Some final questions

About your own career
- Which of the four balances is currently of most concern to
  you?
- If there is an imbalance, what do you believe to be the key
  factors involved? Which of the organisation's or your own
  expectations are out of kilter?
- Was there one particular event which forced this imbalance to
  your attention? What was it? Or are there regular and
  widespread evidences of it?

About your organisation
- On which of the four balances does your organisation concentrate most? Why?
- Does it claim to support the psychological contract (if not in so many words)? The diversity of values? Does it support them in practice?
- Is your organisation's relationship with you reflected in the results of the research I described?

Notes

1 G.M. Robinson (1986) 'Handling cultural diversity', in A. Mumford (ed.), *Handbook of Management Development*, 2nd edn. London: Gower Press.

2 I.E. Sveiby and T. Lloyd (1987) *Managing Know-how*. London: Bloomsbury; M.J. Prietula and H.A. Simon (1989) 'The experts in your midst', *Harvard Business Review*, 89 (1): 120–4.

3 E.H. Schein (1985) *Organisational Culture and Leadership*. San Francisco: Jossey-Bass.

4 P. Herriot, C. Pemberton and R. Pinder (1992) 'Preconditions for the psychological contract', Paper submitted to *Journal of Management Studies*.

5 E.H. Schein (1978) *Career Dynamics: Matching Individual and Organisation Needs*. Reading, Massachusetts: Addison-Wesley.

6 W. Hirsh (1990) *Succession Planning: Current Practice and Future Issues*. Brighton: Institute of Manpower Studies.

7 D.M. Rousseau (1990) 'New hire perceptions of their own and their employer's obligations: A study of psychological contracts', *Journal of Organisational Behaviour*, 11 (5): 389–400.

6

The Rush to Change

Strategies and structures

Striking a series of balances and rushing ahead at breakneck speed are attempted simultaneously only by fools and horses. Organisations are losing their balance because they are being forced (or sometimes are choosing) to pursue precipitate change. Many are currently seeking to reorientate themselves in the market-place; they are shifting towards new business strategies. Others are confident in their current positioning, or cannot summon up the resources or the will to change. So how can we categorise business strategies? And how can we make sense of the currently shifting scene?

The clearest available analysis of strategy is that offered by Miles and Snow.[1] They distinguish four basic strategic types:

- *defenders*, who seal off a market segment and seek to dominate it by competitive efficiency;
- *analysers*, who imitate competitors to get into new markets, but keep a firm base of traditional products or services and customers;
- *prospectors*, who constantly search for new markets and products to develop, and have decentralised administrative systems;
- *reactors*, who are so much at the mercy of their environments that all they can do is to react to events. Survival is their major concern.

To check that these categories make sense, let's think of a couple of archetypal members of each in the UK:

Defender: Tate and Lyle; Tesco.
Analyser: Shell; IBM.
Prospector: Hanson; BAT.
Reactor: London Underground; Mirror Group.

But so profound are the current changes that the picture isn't one of static categories, however neat and helpful. Rather, in response to environmental shifts, many UK organisations themselves are on

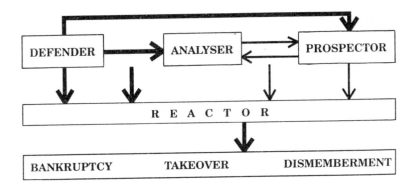

Figure 6.1 *Current strategic shifts*

the move, shifting from one strategic type towards another. Figure 6.1 gives an overview, with arrows of different sizes representing strategic shifts of differing degrees of frequency. Let's consider each in turn.

From defender to analyser
Some public sector and many private sector defenders are being forced to shift. The trend towards greater competition for larger and freer markets has meant that they can't remain competitive merely by increased efficiency. Many would like to develop into analysers, and are culturally suited to doing so. Careful analysis and well-researched decision-making suit their style. And they can still hang on to their core product or service.

From defender to reactor
Many more defenders, though, started to shift too late, and have been forced down by the recession into reactor mode.

From defender to prospector
Some defenders have tried to buy their way out, diversifying rapidly into new markets by acquiring other businesses. Not many have tried to make this shift organically by increased expenditure on research and development into new products and services.

From shifter to reactor
Making strategic shifts is a dangerous undertaking. Organisations are especially vulnerable in such periods of intense change.

From analyser to prospector and the reverse

Some analysers are finding that they are so centralised in their decision-making that innovative and entrepreneurial activity is being stifled; they are hiving off into small prospector organisations. Other small prospectors, often in the hi-tech sector, grow to a point where they feel they need to become analysers.

Again it's good to put some flesh and blood on to these theoretical moves by testing them out against UK organisational reality. Consider, for example, the financial sector.

Many financial organisations are or have been until recently defenders. Some have tried to become prospectors, branching out into a variety of markets because they were available. Many are would-be analysers; but their progress to this hallowed status of the good and the great has been slow, and the recession and increased foreign competition is sending some of them down into reactor mode. A few have failed to move, failed to retain their share of their market, and shot down through reactor mode into being taken over or bankrupted. The same sort of picture can be painted for the textile industry.[2]

These strategic types, and the shifts between them, obviously have consequences for the people who work in them and for the nature of their careers. What effects do these strategic shifts have on people's careers? How can we relate strategic types to human resource systems?

In a brilliant theoretical article Jeffrey Sonnenfeld and Maury Peiperl do just this.[3] Going back to basics, they argue that there are two fundamental properties of career systems in organisations. These are the *supply flow*, the movement into and out of the organisation, and the *assignment flow*, the movement between jobs within the organisation. In terms of the supply flow, some organisations are almost entirely closed to outsiders, except at entry points at the bottom of the hierarchy. They have an internal labour market, and IBM is a good example. Others are open all the way up, and may recruit externally at any level. In terms of the assignment flow, some organisations tend to assign people to jobs on the basis of their individual performance and productivity; other firms will move people on the grounds of their *group* contribution. It's the star performer versus the solid contributor: Kirk and Spock versus Scotty.

Sonnenfeld and Peiperl then construct a 2 × 2 matrix based on these dimensions (see Figure 6.2). Externally recruiting, star-promoting firms are labelled *baseball teams*. Development tends to be on the job, and there's a high turnover, with careers consisting mainly of moves between organisations. Internally recruiting star-promoting firms are called *academies*. These are the organisations which get people early and grow them. We find fast-track schemes and low turnover in these organisations, although some poor performers may leave. The *club* organisation is one which recruits internally and promotes on the basis of group contribution. It places a high value on loyalty, equity and reliability. People move slowly up and through these organisations, and tend to develop as generalists rather than specialists. Finally, we have the *fortresses*. These are firms with an external recruiting policy, high turnover with much redundancy, and little commitment to employees. Survival is their concern, and they allocate positions to counter short-term threats or to restructure for the future.

External labour market	FORTRESS	BASEBALL TEAM
Internal labour market	CLUB	ACADEMY

Group contribution ———— Individual contribution

Figure 6.2 *A model of career systems*

Source: Sonnenfeld and Peiperl (1988)

For the baseball team, the emphasis is on *recruitment*; for the academy, *development*; for the club, *retention*; and for the fortress, *retrenchment*.

Now we can relate these four types of career system to the four strategic types (see Figure 6.3).

STRATEGIC TYPE	Prospector	Analyser	Defender	Reactor
CAREER SYSTEM	Baseball team	Academy	Club	Fortress
CAREER PRIORITY	Recruitment	Development	Retention	Retrenchment

Figure 6.3 *Matching of strategy, systems and priorities*

Source: based on Sonnenfeld and Peiperl (1988)

Firms with a *prospector* strategy will tend to have a *baseball team* career system. They move into new markets and products rapidly, seizing opportunities as they come up. Consequently they attract stars to give them a competitive edge by developing new products and services, or by taking over and turning round new acquisitions.

Analysers will probably be *academies*. Analysers think carefully before going into new markets or products. They are not always at the cutting edge of innovation. Rather, they creatively ensure the reliable production and delivery of high-quality new products or services. Consequently, they need the academy system to provide them with people who will carry through these well-researched projects. They need people who have specific expertise but who also understand the organisation and its business. That's why they recruit young and promote internally.

Defender organisations will probably be *clubs*. Defenders want to maintain themselves in a particular market rather than expanding. They will sometimes have a monopoly and be protected from competition by regulation. They may provide a highly valued service to the community, and be in the public rather than the private sector. Consequently, they grow from within people who contribute loyally to the general corporate aims.

Finally, *reactors* will be like *fortresses*. Buffeted by their environment, reacting to it rather than anticipating, they will retrench. This often involves bringing in a new top management team and making many people redundant. They need both to reduce costs and to increase productivity, and people are a major cost. So fortresses tend to recruit externally a new top team and cheap replacement labour. They have little time for temperamental stars – it's all hands to the pump.

It's not hard to allocate organisations and, indeed, sectors, to these four types. *Defender clubs*, for example, could include the Civil Service, the armed services, the Royal Mail, and some of the larger banks and insurance companies. *Analyser academies* number among them the good and the great – ICI, Shell, BP, IBM, Marks & Spencer. Many organisations become *reactor fortresses* when they get into difficulties. Often this is in the transition from being a defender club to another type. *Prospector baseball teams* will include many small hi-tech consultancy or professional firms; entertainment, public relations, or advertising firms. We may also include some of the large conglomerates, who by acquisition and divestment move rapidly into and out of markets as opportunities develop and new markets present themselves. Here there is a mixed form: a central prospecting baseball team often sending out players into reactor fortresses to turn them around.

But it's not the static allocation of organisations to categories that we're interested in. Rather it is the dynamic movements between strategic types. The great strategic shifts of our time are:

- from defender clubs to analyser academies;
- from defender clubs to prospector baseball teams;
- from any type of shift down into reactor fortresses.

Therefore the shifts in HR strategy tend to be:

- towards an external labour market (except for analyser academies);
- towards an individual emphasis (except for reactor fortresses).

We can see these trends in evidence almost daily. Continued job losses emphasise the insecurity of employment in all sectors as organisations move into reactor fortress mode. Prospector baseball teams recruit from analyser academies on the basis of star innovative potential, while the latter still try to retain individuals by developing them through a planned career. Prospectors and reactors search for hero executives from outside who can turn new acquisitions or the organisation around. But the biggest consequence of all these shifts is a loss of balance; and the first casualty is Scotty. For the shift from defender has seen the loss of the loyalty – security contract.

Culture change programmes

These strategic changes in the HR function are profound. Externalising their labour markets and concentrating on individuals are major shifts for some organisations. Yet organisations are finding that this is not enough. Strategic and structural shifts by themselves often fail to achieve the degree of overall change necessary to meet the demands of the new business environment. Despite major shake-ups, organisations still feel that they are lagging behind. Many have come to realise that strategies and structure are only part of the change required. Other, deeper aspects of the culture such as values and assumptions also need to change.

The response of some organisations on reaching this conclusion is to set up culture change programmes. Alan Williams and colleagues surveyed 1,000 major UK organisations, and found that more than 250 had been involved in the previous five years in conscious attempts to change their cultures.[4] Typically, these attempts involved trying to change internal events in organisations in response to some major external event (such as deregulation). What form do these culture change programmes take?

Chris Hendry, Andrew Pettigrew and Paul Sparrow looked at 20 UK organisations during the 1980s.[5] Five were in the computer industry (computers or services), 6 manufacturing and engineering, 2 banks, 2 retail, 2 public sector, and 3 others in the service sector. They ranged in size from 48 to 75,000 employees. They certainly changed radically, both externally and internally during this period. Of the 20, 13 experienced changes in their top leadership, and 13 had been through major redundancy programmes. Many of these organisations made conscious efforts to change their culture, in two specific directions. They tried to focus attention on performance; and/or they tried to introduce a customer or a total quality orientation.

The emphasis on performance is gaining momentum at present, and there is no reason to suppose that it will not continue through the 1990s. The main engine for change is human resource systems, in particular the rewards system. The most common practice is to make a certain proportion of salary contingent upon an individual's performance. This is often assessed annually by an appraisal procedure in which various aspects of performance are rated by the individual's line manager. Various methods of monitoring and managing performance are introduced as well.

Some organisations describe themselves as having a performance culture. This implies that excellence of performance is a value which is held to be far above all others in the organisation. During the 90s, those organisations seeking to reinforce such a culture will organise their human resource systems so as to support it. An overall HR 'system of systems' to reinforce a performance culture is given in Figure 6.4. Clearly, this 'human resource cycle' is centred around performance as the key concept. Recruitment and selection are aimed at employing those who will perform well. Appraisal is of performance, and leads to performance-related rewards and to training. Rewards and training are designed to improve performance further. Development prepares people for selection to new jobs in which their performance will be appraised, and so on. Obviously one of the current strategic HR emphases, that on the individual, is being reinforced by performance programmes. What of customer care programmes?

A brief case study can perhaps give us a flavour. One of the best known recent examples in the UK is that of British Airways (more fully described by Charles Hampden-Turner).[6] In 1983, BA made a loss of £100 million and a new chief executive and human resource director were appointed. They sought to understand the nature of the existing culture, which was derived from the Royal Air Force background of previous senior management. In particular, they

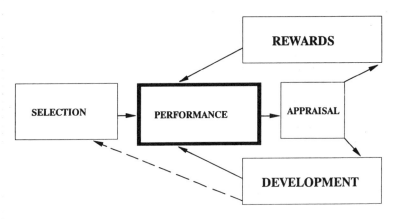

Figure 6.4 *The human resource cycle*

noted the ubiquitous signals of rank and the large numbers of rules
and regulations that permeated the organisation. They realised that
these and other aspects of the culture were militating against
providing for customers the individualised service which might give
BA a competitive edge and make it the airline of first rather than
last choice. They started by interviewing cabin staff, the people
who actually provided service face to face. They discovered these
front-line staff experienced various value conflicts. They wanted to
provide flexible service but didn't want to break the rules which
prevented them from doing so. They wanted to meet BA's expectations, but found that these conflicted frequently with their obligations at home. Systemic changes were made which removed these
dilemmas; many rules were abolished and shifts were allocated to
take account of domestic responsibilities.

But a more potent conflict soon emerged. The cabin staff
perceived themselves to be receiving less support from their
managers than they themselves were now giving to customers. The
hierarchical nature of the culture prevented managers from perceiv-
ing their role as supportive. A training programme was introduced
for them with this objective, and furthermore, the Chief Executive
insisted on the removal of various signals of rank. When addressed
as 'CX' (Chief Executive), he told his subordinate to call him by
his name, and this event rapidly became an organisational myth
which signalled a value change. The process of change at BA
continues, and Hampden-Turner suggests that it might still be
meeting resistance at middle management level.

This example provides us with some interesting questions. Was
the organisational change programme reactive or proactive? It was

reactive in the sense that it was the indirect consequence of poor financial performance; it was proactive in that customer service was selected as the single value priority which would make BA competitive in the long run. Was the programme imposed from above, or was it a reflection of an organisation-wide movement? It was imposed from above in the sense that it was a consciously planned strategy devised by senior management. But it reflected one of the value priorities of that large part of the workforce which interacted with the customer. It could be argued that the pro-gramme empowered cabin crew by enabling them to resolve several of the value conflicts they were experiencing, and by giving them more responsibility to take their own decisions.

The example also raises interesting questions about how the change happened. Systems, behaviour and stated value priorities *all* changed, but in no discernible sequence. It wasn't assumed, for example, that:

- in order to change behaviour, attitudes have to change first;
- change the systems, and the rest will automatically follow;
- change has to start at the more senior levels to be successful.

British Airways, in other words, didn't fall into the *rationalistic* fallacy: that people always choose what they will do on the basis of their values. They realised that people act as they do for all sorts of reasons: because the situation makes it easy for them to act in that way, because other people are acting in that way, and so on. Nor did BA fall into the *mechanistic* fallacy: change the structure or the systems and people will act differently. Nor, finally, did it fall for the *power* fallacy – that people at the top of the hierarchy determine what goes on at the grass-roots level. On the contrary, BA realised that only concerted efforts at change in a variety of modes and at a variety of hierarchical levels had a hope of success.

Many attempts at cultural engineering are far more coercive than this. Instead of discovering employees' value conflicts and trying to support them as they are resolved, many have tried to impose value priorities from above. These often take the form of vision or mission statements under the name of the Chief Executive. As Schein notes, 'formal statements cannot be seen as a way of defin-ing the culture of an organisation. At best they cover a small, publicly relevant segment of the culture, those aspects that leaders find useful to publish as an ideology for the organisation.'[7] Other organisational change attempts are totally reactive. New structure and systems are introduced in response to a crisis, but behaviour, values and assumptions are not addressed – they are assumed to follow on automatically. The consequence is that practice on the ground doesn't change at all. This is the result of unilateral top-down statements of vision or changes in structure and systems. And a final difficulty with most culture change attempts is that they seek to introduce simple, 'strong' cultures. These are often statements of a single all-embracing value priority – to meet customers' needs; to ensure total quality performance; to be an international market leader. The variety of environmental pressures and of employees' own value priorities render such simplistic solutions unlikely to succeed in any terms.

A recent piece of research by Michael Beer and colleagues supports my argument.[8] Provocatively entitling their article 'Why change programs don't produce change', they demonstrate in a review of six conscious attempts at change, that success occurs when:

- change starts in a small way at the periphery of the organisation;
- it is concerned to tackle the organisation's most important competitive task;
- it is primarily focused on roles, responsibilities and relationships, not on the behaviour or attitudes of individuals in isolation;
- it is specifically adapted to particular units, rather than monolithic across the organisation.

In sum, successful attempts at change concentrate on current business issues rather than taking attention away from them. If this is a necessary condition for success, it means that change attempts have to be reactive rather than proactive.

How far do these current culture change efforts go in achieving our four balances and the two meta-values which underpin them (see pp. 67–72)? The first balance between organisational expectations of adventure and exploration and individual expectations of support implied that a high value was placed on responsiveness to change; risk and innovation; tolerance of failure; development of people; and supportive teamwork. Current emphasis on change towards performance and customer first certainly values change itself. It *may* support risk and innovation if employees are given the responsibility for responding to client needs themselves. On the other hand, an emphasis on measured performance can inhibit innovation, since you know you can achieve certain levels if you carry on as at present (but with a bit more effort!). Tolerance of failure is likely to be low, and development of people will be valued only in so far as it meets specific objectives of performance improvement or customer care. Finally, if the performance culture values and rewards individual performance, then it is likely to militate against supportive teamwork.

The second balancing act was between organisational demands of loyalty and commitment and individual expectations of their individual rights. We suggested that honouring agreements, mutual loyalty, respecting rights, deserving rewards, respecting individuality, making agreements explicit, and experience and organisational knowledge will be highly valued in an organisational culture which achieves this balance. Customer first and performance cultures seem fairly neutral on most of these. If employees are included as 'customers', then some mutuality enters the picture. And certainly, the performance culture makes agreements explicit and tries to ensure that rewards are deserved. On the other hand, coercive attempts to change people's values to embrace a single 'strong' value priority may violate individuals' rights and negate their individuality.

The third balancing act is likely to require a high value to be placed on core competencies, on stars, and on communication and collaboration. Again, while a performance culture also values stars, it may not foster communication and collaboration if it focuses upon individual performance only.

The fourth and final balance is that between the corporate needs for information and control and individuals' expectations of autonomy and trust. Local knowledge, boundary people, communication of strategy and innovative local initiatives should be valued. Customer-first cultures should actively promote local knowledge and boundary people, but single value cultures may not favour local initiatives.

Most important, single value 'strong' cultures and their coercive introduction contradict both of our meta-values. A high value placed on diversity of values is clearly incompatible with such single value cultures. So is the psychological contract, since it implies a two-way negotiated agreement geared to both parties' needs, not an imposed culture. In summary the attempt to implement strategy by means of conscious attempts to change organisational culture goes only part of the way towards achieving the balancing act of the 90s. Particularly with respect to the values of collaboration, diversity of values and the psychological contract, cultural engineering is moving in the opposite direction.

The human resource movement

There is a second push to use HR people to try to ensure that strategy is implemented. It is revealed in the use of the term 'human resources' instead of 'personnel', and of the ultimate accolade 'strategy'. Two main criteria must be met if a human resource strategy is to be achieved. First, HR systems have to be integrated to achieve strategic aims. (Figure 6.4 illustrates systems integration to serve the strategic aims of performance management.) Secondly, HR professionals have to be involved in strategic planning at organisational level.[9] According to Chris Hendry and Andrew Pettigrew the key competences of HR professionals are likely to involve broad training and experience across the full range of HRM activities, the capability to link business and technical changes to HRM considerations along with the conceptual ability to think in business and HRM terms, and the development of process skills inside firms to produce the necessary changes.[10] They go on to insist that the crucial difference between 'personnel' and the new breed of HR professional is the ability to take, and implement, a strategic view of the whole range of personnel practices in relation to business activity as a whole. In terms of current trends, for example, they might be advising on whether it's feasible to develop a new core organisational competence.

Other UK writers are not so clear about this new direction. Roger Cooke and Michael Armstrong, for example, warn that the concept of strategic human resource management is in danger of becoming an apple-pie idea of which we are all in favour.[11] They argue that 'although relatively few strategic HR issues arise at corporate level, those that do may be decisive. They include the organisation's mission; its values, culture and style; management as a corporate resource; and the management of change.' Cooke and Armstrong argue that HR strategy has to be 'emergent', to use Henry Mintzberg's word.[12] In other words, it has to be flexible, rapidly adjusting to change in brief quantum leaps.

Given the broad scope of HR strategy as defined by these authors (what organisation's prime task *isn't* to manage change?) the implication seems to be that we shouldn't distinguish HR from business strategy. Rather, the two should be completely integrated, since organisational change and culture are inseparable from such supposedly 'business' issues as mergers and acquisitions. Indeed, total integration of HR and business strategy is the final state of grace in the development of the HR function. Karen Golden and Vasudevan Ramanujam argue for the following sequence of development.[13] At the most primitive level of development there is simply an administrative linkage between HR and strategic planning. The HR function fulfils the traditional personnel role, providing day-to-day operational support. The next stage involves a one-way linkage, in which HR designs programmes and systems to support the organisation's strategic objectives. Two-way linkage, the next stage, implies a reciprocal and interdependent relationship between HR and strategic planning. HR personnel are proactive in responding to and helping determine the firm's strategic direction – they are strategic partners with line managers and planners. Finally, in a totally integrative linkage, the HR director is involved with top management in all strategic decisions, even when they may not apparently involve HR concerns.

Paul Buller examined eight US organisations, all of which were highly regarded in the USA for their advanced management practices.[14] None were at the administrative level, three had a one-way linkage, three a two-way, and two were entirely integrated. Looking at these latter two specifically, Buller noted that in one of them the vice-president for human resources made explicit his philosophy that 'we're here to help the company make a profit'. All who aspired to reach HR management had to have general business experience. In the other integrated organisation, the senior corporate HR job was the stepping-stone to the top position.

Buller looked at those factors which tended to push organisations towards integration. Organisations which faced particular increases in their competition, technological change, and more varied employees, were further along the developmental path. Diversification into unrelated business areas, on the other hand, made integration less likely. In the more integrated organisations the senior HR executive was perceived to have business awareness and reported directly to the Chief Executive. These organisations also communicated strategic plans to managers, and operated well-developed HR databases.

Buller concludes with the usual 'contingency' statement – that is, he suggests that different levels of integration are appropriate for organisations in different situations. 'The data suggested that higher levels of integration may be necessary for firms operating in dynamic environments, whereas lower levels of integration may be appropriate for those in stable environments.' This contingency approach is echoed by other writers. Ilan Meshoulam and Lloyd Baird, for example,[15] argue on the basis of their investigation of thirty US organisations that the level of HR development should mesh with the stage of development of the organisation as a whole; is the organisation at the initiation, functional growth, controlled growth, functional integration, or strategic integration stages? If the HR function lags behind or surges ahead of this general level of development it is less effective.

All of these contingency theories laudably recognise the differences that exist between organisations. But if my argument in this book is correct, there are certain environmental features which are currently affecting and will in future affect, most medium and large organisations: these include increased competition, information technology, globalisation of markets, and takeovers and mergers. It is these near-universal dynamic forces towards change which make the move towards HR integration a *general* rather than a *contingent* probability.

The examples we have considered so far are from the USA. A recent European research project sponsored jointly by Price Waterhouse and Cranfield School of Management looked at strategic HR management in five European countries.[16] There was very little agreement on what best HR practices were – for example, the extent to which HR responsibilities should be exercised by line management, or the degree of 'welfare' orientation appropriate for an HR function. However, a general movement *was* reported towards a pivotal role for HR involving:

- HR influence at strategic level;
- coherent and consistent HR policies;
- adaptability of these policies to circumstances;
- added value from the HR function to the organisation;
- evaluation of results.

In terms of influence at strategic level, the UK tended to have somewhat less representation of HR at board level than Sweden, France and Spain. The UK degree of representation, however (63 per cent) far exceeded that of Germany (19 per cent). This may partly be due to different legal requirements, but argues against a facile assumption that more HR influence leads to better business performance (in which Germany is not exactly a laggard!). In terms of actual influence on business strategy, some 44 per cent of the UK HR directors sampled are involved from the outset. Also noteworthy were responses to the question: 'In what areas of personnel responsibility has line management influence increased?' Training and development, recruitment and selection, and pay and benefits were the areas most frequently cited, as part of a general trend towards devolving the determination and implementation of policy to line managers. Personnel professionals are used as consultants by line managers, so the integration of HR with the business appears to be taking place at strategic and operational levels in Europe as well as in America.

Looking further afield than America and Europe, we find quite a wide diversity of HR practice. A.M. Jaeger and R.N. Kanungo urge us not to assume that HR strategies developed for industrialised societies will be appropriate for developing countries.[17] Such strategies will be effective only when they mesh in with local cultures, they argue, and cite the huge differences which are to be found along Hofstede's dimensions (see pp. 37–8). Clearly, notions of planning are alien to cultures which tolerate uncertainty without difficulty, while organisational structural changes separate individuals from their existing face-to-face relationships.

How likely is it that the move in the West towards strategic HR management will bring about the balances between organisational and individual expectations described at the beginning of this chapter? How much difference will it make to the behaviour, values, systems and structure of an organisation if an HR professional is on the board? And, if it does make a difference, is that difference going to be towards or away from our desired balances? Certainly, HR directors will have no difficulty in demonstrating that the organisation must have added expectations of employees if it is to survive and compete. Everyone realises that their Kirks, Spocks, Scotties and Uhuras are indispensible crew members. And this very indispensibility will enable HR directors to press for better recruitment and reward systems designed to attract and retain them. But will HR directors broaden their vision to look from the individual's as well as the organisation's point of view? And if they do have that breadth of vision, will others on the board share it? Will they realise its implications for the loss of much of their power? And will they, despite that realisation, have the courage to broaden the scope of their psychological contract with their employees so as to achieve it? Your answer is as good as mine; but what's sure is that the survivors and the winners will be those organisations which respect the talents, the preferences and the rights of their members.

So in this chapter the absence of a psychological contract, or indeed, of many of the preconditions for its existence, which we saw evidenced in chapter 5, has been set in its context. The frequent absence of our four key balances and of the two overarching values is partly attributable to the breakneck speed at which many organisations are trying to change their business strategy. Programmes of culture change and the human resources movement are both attempts to recover balance; the former by short sharp shock, the latter by longer-term integration of HR with the business. Both often fail the litmus test of the two overarching values: valuing diversity and a reciprocal relationship with employees.

Some final questions

About your own career

- Have you worked for organisations of different strategic types during your working life? What were the differences in the way different types dealt with your career? How did you feel about each?
- If your organisation is currently shifting, how do you feel about your career prospects? Explore further any anxieties you may feel – what are the beliefs underlying them?
- What effects did any culture change programme you have experienced have on you personally?

About your organisation

- Does your organisation fit into one strategic type? Or is it on the move? If so, which shift is it currently making?
- If your organisation fits into one type, does its HR strategy accord with Figure 6.3?
- If it's shifting, what effects is the shift having on the HR strategy – towards individuals? towards an external labour market?
- Has your organisation engaged in a conscious culture change programme? How did it start? Who championed it? How was it conducted? By whom? What were the outcomes?
- At what stage of integration is your HR function: administrative, one-way, two-way or totally integrated? Why is it at that stage?

Notes

1 R.E. Miles and C.C. Snow (1978) *Organizational Strategy, Structure, and Process*. New York: McGraw Hill.

2 N. Nicholson, A. Rees and A. Brooks-Rooney (1990) 'Strategy, innovation and performance', *Journal of Management Studies*, 27 (5): 511–34.

3 J. Sonnenfeld and M. Peiperl (1988) 'Staffing policy as a strategic response: a typology of career systems', *Academy of Management Review*, 13 (4): 588–600.

4 A. Williams, P. Dobson and M. Walters (1989) *Changing Culture*. London: IPM Press.

5 C. Hendry, A. Pettigrew and P. Sparrow (1988) 'Changing patterns of human resource management', *Personnel Management*, 20 (11): 37–41.

6 C. Hampden-Turner (1990) *Corporate Culture: Vicious to Virtuous Circles*. London: Hutchinson.

7 E.H. Schein (1985) *Organisational Culture and Leadership*. San Francisco: Jossey-Bass. p. 242.

8 M. Beer, R.A. Eisenstat and B. Spector (1990) 'Why change programs don't produce change', *Harvard Business Review*, 68 (61): 158–66.

9 C. Fombrun, N.M. Tichy and M.A. Devanna (eds) (1984) *Strategic Human Resource Management*. New York: John Wiley.

10 C. Hendry and A. Pettigrew (1987) 'Banking on HRM to respond to change', *Personnel Management*, 19 (11): 33–6.

11 R. Cooke and M. Armstrong (1990) 'The search for strategic HRM', *Personnel Management*, 22 (12): 30–3.

12 J.B. Quinn, H. Mintzberg and R.M. James (1988) *The Strategy Process: Concepts, Contexts, and Cases*. Englewood Cliffs, NJ: Prentice-Hall.

13 K. Golden and V. Ramanujam (1985) 'Between a dream and a nightmare: on the integration of the human resource management and the strategic business planning process', *Human Resources Management*, 24: 46–58.

14 P. Buller (1988) 'Successful partnerships: HR and strategic planning at eight top firms', *Organisational Dynamics*, 1988 (Spring): 27–43.

15 I. Meshoulam and L. Baird (1987) 'Proactive human resource management', *Human Resource Management*, 26 (4): 483–502.

16 *The Price Waterhouse Cranfield Project on International Strategic Human Resource Management* (1990). London: Price Waterhouse.

17 A.M. Jaeger and R.N. Kanungo (1990) (eds) *Management in Developing Countries*. London: Routledge.

7

Change and Support

Managerial work and competencies

Poor old Tyrannosaurus paid the price. He didn't change as fast as his environment, so he died off. Organisations which survive to the end of the decade will be *by definition*, organisations which have changed. The change will be a total one, in the sense that all aspects of the culture will be different: assumptions, values, behaviour and systems. Change may be the result of a conscious one-off programme. It will, more probably, be a continuous process, sometimes anticipating, sometimes responding to outside events. Either way, it will have to emulate the British Airways process described on pp. 88–90. That is, it will have to involve all of the four pillars of change: assumptions, values, behaviour and systems. Systems because they facilitate and support what people do; behaviour, because unless people change what they do, little else changes; values, because changes in behaviour need to be motivated beforehand and justified afterwards; assumptions, because behaviour and values need to fit into the overall framework we use to make sense and give meaning to our world. Behaviour change without the value and assumption changes to underpin it is temporary and unreliable. It depends on the presence of immediate external factors: the threat of punishment (such as dismissal), the promise of reward (for example bonus payments), or the presence of an inspiring model (a charismatic boss). As soon as the promises and threats are removed, or the boss moves on, the behaviour changes. It isn't *internalised* and supported by values and assumptions.

So it is what people do that really matters; systems are (supposed to be) there to help them; values and assumptions are necessary conditions for behaviour change to last. But values have another highly important function: they can be communicated easily. It's not hard to tell others what you think is important around here; nor is it impossible to admit that the people across the corridor may rightly believe one or two other things are important as well. This is why I focused so strongly upon values in chapter 5. Changing systems and structures alone is merely tinkering; it is hard to discuss behaviour in sufficiently general terms to refer to the whole organisation; while assumptions are very difficult to discover and bring into the open. Nevertheless, we need to consider all of these elements of change together in our efforts to foresee the shape of things to come by the end of the decade.

The first balance which will have been struck by the year 2000 by surviving organisations is that between the expectation of change and adventure by the organisation and that of development and support by employees. To recapitulate, the values necessary to achieve this balance were that a high priority should be given to

- responsiveness to change;
- risk and innovation;
- tolerance of failures;
- development of people;
- supportive teamwork.

The underlying assumptions were that

- people can change;
- people can like change;
- people need help;
- people help each other;
- organisation is there to support people.

What behavioural and systemic changes will accompany these changed values and assumptions? What will be the differences in what people do and in the systems that support them?

The fact is, it's extraordinarily difficult to discover what people do at work. Most of those jobs which involve predictable sequences of tasks that are programmable have already been programmed. More and more people find themselves working to solve problems to which there is no single tried and tested existing solution. And the problems with which they are faced are changing in nature all the time as a consequence of the major business changes outlined in chapter 2:

- People have to be persuaded rather than told to do things.
- Customers are becoming more demanding.
- New markets require new solutions.
- New technology changes the way work is done.
- Additional responsibilities need new skills.
- Integrated product or service provision needs collaboration.
- Internationalisation and takeover raise people problems.

One response to all this change is to describe people's work in terms of their current responsibilities and the people to whom they are accountable for various outcomes, regardless of *how* they fulfil them. Obviously, this misses out on what they do. Further, it is a very 'official' view of work – its formalisation tends to obscure the fact that lots of different people expect things of job holders, and that they in turn expect a lot from a variety of others inside and outside the organisation.

Nowhere has the task of describing what people do been more difficult than in the area of managerial work. Henry Mintzberg in the USA and Rosemary Stewart in the UK found that the episodes in a manager's working day were nasty, brutish and short.[1] Their work seemed to be terribly fragmented, and the only way the researchers could make sense of it was in terms of various roles (such as monitor, resource allocator, disturbance handler and figurehead) between which they switched. One of the troubles with this approach, of course, is that the researchers are imposing their meaning on what the manager is doing. Although the manager may do a series of apparently different things – talk to a subordinate, fix an appointment, plan a budget – these may all be linked in his or her own mind. The manager may construe these activities as all contributing to a more general objective. So to say that managers will be doing different things in different proportions in ten years' time is not very helpful. To say that they will be construing their work and its objectives in a new way *is* helpful; it will enable us to look deeper than the surface of their behaviour. We'll be able to say, for example, how they will feel they are organising their work, and to what ends.

There is a currently popular alternative scenario. Perhaps we should be talking in terms of what *competencies* employees will be needing. The idea itself is rather hard to pin down – are we talking about underlying characteristics of a person, about their potential for a certain level of performance, or about their actual performance set against some criterion? Perhaps some examples will help. British Petroleum uses four clusters of competencies:[2] achievement orientation cluster, which includes personal drive, organisational drive, impact and communication as the individual competencies; people orientation, including awareness of others, team management and persuasiveness; judgement, including analytical power, strategic thinking and commercial judgement; and situational flexibility incorporating only adaptive orientation. Each competence is defined; for example drive is said to be 'self-confident and assertive drive to win, with decisiveness and resilience'. Rating scales of 1 (high) to 5 are provided, with descriptions for each point of the scale. Point 1 reads 'Decisive even under pressure, assertive and tough-minded in arguing his/her case, very self-confident, shrugs off setbacks.' A rating of 5 is for one who 'doesn't pursue his/her points, goes along with the group, allows criticism or setbacks to deter him/her'. Those who score high are said to be likely to have the following strengths:

- tough-minded, results oriented;
- comfortable with decision-making;
- faces conflicts;
- strong-willed;
- great faith in self;
- will take charge;
- determined to achieve;
- comfortable in competitive settings.

On the other hand, it is recognised that someone high in personal drive may have corresponding development needs – for example, he or she may need to learn to be less aggressive, more of a team player, more amenable to others' ideas, less confident. In other words, such a person would need to learn to avoid being seen only as a tough battler. Someone low on personal drive would have certain corresponding strengths, for example:

- sacrificing own interests for good of whole;
- tactful, manages conflict situations;
- open to influence;
- comfortable in collaborative settings.

This individual may, from a developmental point of view, need to learn to make decisions, to face confrontation and competition and to challenge.

These descriptions imply relative strengths and weaknesses for both high and low scorers, and so, on the face of it, neither a high nor a low score is more desirable. The game is given away, how-ever, by the use of the phrase ' + indicators' to head a list of characteristics of high scorers, and ' – indicators' for low scorers. In other words, the organisation values highly the sort of behaviour which results from high personal drive. This is fine, provided that this value is up-front and explicit. Whether *in general* it is an appropriate value for the 90s is another question. Does BP want all of its managers to be high on personal drive, with the universally individualistic behaviour that this implies? Does it want such behaviour to be exhibited in *all* the situations and problems its managers face?

These questions point to two of the major criticisms of the typical use of competencies by large UK organisations. First, they are too generalised: they are supposed to apply across managerial work in general within the organisation. Not only this: it is proposed that a generic set of competencies is applicable to managerial work in general (though with different emphases at different levels of management). These proposals by such as Boyatzis and Schroder assume that managerial work is similar across different organisations in different sectors in different cultures.[3]

So attractive is this proposition at first sight that it formed the cornerstone of the attempt to professionalise management by the Management Charter group, as reported by Mike Day.[4] If competencies are common to all managerial work, then various levels of professional accreditation can be given to those demonstrating various levels of competence. Professionalisation may or may not be the best way to improve the quality of British management. After all, the most powerful professions are noted for paying more attention to their own than to their clients' interests. But, more importantly, is it meaningful to speak of 'management' as a profession at all? Has the question ever been asked 'Is there a manager in the house?' Does the title 'chartered manager' ring the same bell as 'chartered accountant'? Mike Day alleges that 'Recent research by the Institute of Manpower Studies concludes that a common language of competence is possible and, if widely accepted would be useful.'[5] What he doesn't mention is that this research, by Wendy Hirsh and Stephen Bevan, found that although some of the same *terms* were used in the assessment documentation of UK companies, they were used with a wide array of different *meanings*.[6]

Much of what the Management Charter Initiative (MCI) is doing will be of great benefit. The concentration on what people can do, and on their previous experience and learning, is timely and welcome. However, the underlying assumption of generic competencies is their Achilles heel.

A second criticism of the idea of competencies seems to contradict the first. I have criticised them for being too generalised, across situation, level, organisation, sector and national culture. Now we will raise the problem of their being too atomistic. They break up individuals into parts, with no indication of how these parts are integrated into successful performance. It is people who perform successfully in social situations, not competencies that are exercised. We have to consider people in the round, people with emotions, values, and identities; and we have to put them into a social and organisational context.

However, the atomisation of the individual isn't just into competencies. Each competency has a set of units, for example the generic competence of 'people orientation' subsumes the unit 'oral communication'. These units are again subdivided into elements, for example 'communicating orally to one other person'. Elements are then defined by a small set of performance criteria statements, against which individuals may be assessed. The statements for the element 'communicating orally with one other person' are:

- demonstrates that intended actions are clearly understood and summarised by the listener;
- provides the amount of information judged to be adequate by the listener;
- provides the listener with information which is orderly, concise and relevant.

It is easy to ridicule these earnest attempts to treat social behaviour as though it were a substance composed of elements of ever-decreasing size. The consequence of doing so is the American Management Association's published regulation:

> In order to complete the program, students are required both to demonstrate competencies during assessment as well as to submit documentation that they have used the competencies on the job . . . . The competencies must be demonstrated a minimum of 32 times during assessment, and they must be documented a minimum of 22 times on the job . . . in order to earn the Master of Management degree.[7]

To be fair, neither of the reports which led up to the Management Charter movement suggested that competencies were common across organisations except at the most basic and junior levels in financial and personal skills.[8] Nor do the organisational users assume a common set of Meccano pieces. On the contrary, they stress that their competencies are couched in language specific to their organisation. Tony Glaze of Cadbury Schweppes, for example, says that in his organisation 'the most fundamental effect . . . has been their contribution to the behavioural literacy of many of our managers'.[9] In other words, Glaze found that the language of Cadbury Schweppes competencies allowed people to think and talk about work in behavioural as well as technical and financial terms.

A final problem arises with regard to the mode of assessment of the competencies and the use to which they are put. This is over-whelmingly in terms of the interests and administrative power of the organisation. Tony Glaze, for example, writes, 'we have been trying to find better ways of describing managers. Our aim has been to store data on them in a more systematic way, enabling *us* to make more effective decisions about *their* future.'[10] Some organisations, for example BP, emphasise that the outcome of assessments of competence is feedback to the assessees where 'not only is feedback given but also discussion of the implications in terms of training, personal development and overall career development, with a strong focus on self-development'.[11] However, even where such development is discussed, it may be development in the interests of the organisation. In Tony Cockerill's description of the widely acclaimed National Westminster Bank's scheme, for example, staff are encouraged to create their own development plans.[12] There are three such plans:

- to make a better contribution to the organisation with their strengths;
- to compensate for their limitations;
- to develop one or two limitations into strengths.

'All three plans include ways of measuring whether development is occurring and whether this is raising the level of organisational performance.'

At least the National Westminster scheme doesn't assess competencies only; it looks at individuals' preferred styles of operating and at career anchors (see pp. 59–60). It also seeks to avoid the somewhat static nature of competencies. They are usually derived from senior managers' reports on what competencies subordinates' jobs require now. These jobs will change in the future as a consequence of the business trends described in chapter 2. The National Westminster Bank therefore adopted a list of competencies demonstrated by Harry Schroder to be characteristic of successful managers in changing organisations.[13] These include such competencies as:

- information search: environmental scanning;
- conceptual flexibility: considers alternatives simultaneously;
- interpersonal search: explores and understands others' viewpoints;
- managing interaction: involves others, builds teams;
- developmental orientation: helps others develop.

Overall, it seems unlikely that competencies will adequately express what employees will be doing by the end of the 90s. Some of them (for example, those cited above from Schroder) incorporate many of the key expectations which organisations will be holding of employees. But the balance will be between organisational and individual expectations; it will not be concerned only with what individuals can do for organisations.

In the end, we must ask ourselves whether there is a basic contradiction in the assessment of individual performance by means of competencies. If managing involves getting things done through and with others, then assessing individual rather than group performance is nonsense. To narrow the search for managerial effectiveness to individual outputs would destroy the concept of management itself.

Another recent attempt to characterise the behaviour of the future is in terms of *managerial style*. Given the changing environment of the 90s, Graham Prentice argues that the typical competitive, action-oriented and autonomous style of the 80s is inappropriate.[14] Managers instead will need to be listening, supportive and empathetic. As Prentice maintains, 'all the characteristics of the future organisation demand a stronger behavioural and supportive management . . .'.

One wonders, though, whether the concept of 'style' adds anything to the notion of putting a set of value priorities into practice. Perhaps all one can say in the end about organisational behaviour of the 90s is that it will express the value priorities of our first balancing act (see p. 69). Indeed, the notion of style may detract from such true expression, since the word implies the opposite of substance: managers may carry on doing the same old things, but doing them in a kindly way!

What is of interest is the concentration of writers and practitioners on managers. Prentice wrote of managerial style, and the Management Charter Initiative is about managerial competencies. We discussed the nature of managerial work. This is a profoundly limiting and retrogressive way of thinking: it equates individuals at certain levels of the organisational hierarchy ('managers') with a particular type of activity ('managing'). It then allocates responsibility for organisational values, systems and behaviour to these individuals, and it provides developmental opportunities to help them shoulder this responsibility. If there is one thing which successful organisational change has taught us, it is that the impetus for change comes from the bottom of the hierarchy as well as from the top. Indeed it is often middle managers who are most resistant to change. The surviving organisations of the year 2000 will treat everyone as having development needs. They will recognise that everyone 'manages', since everyone has responsibilities for others and gets things done by enlisting their help. And they will understand that the equating of 'the organisation's' values with those of senior management is a grave error.

Development

So what sort of development will be available in the year 2000? How will the values of responsiveness to change, development of people and supportive teamwork be expressed in organisational systems? How will the assumptions that people can change and that the organisation is there to support people be worked out in practice? The Management Charter group has given us a splendid vision for the future. If only they had stuck to this notion of a charter (or contract) between organisation and employee, instead of trying to establish a *chartered* profession of management on the basis of competencies. All organisations belonging to the Charter group subscribe to the following principles (among others):

- *Management development – a prime corporate objective*: We are dedicated to the sustained success of our organisation by making the most of the existing talents and future potential of each employee. To this end, we will translate our corporate objectives and the related plans into complementary programmes for the development of our managers *at all levels throughout the organisation.*
- *The means – systematic self-development*: We will encourage all practising and aspiring managers to engage in individual programmes of continuous self-development, each consistent with the best interests of the organisation. In adapting the organisation in response to change, we will strive both to enhance its performance and, where possible, to reinforce this by providing suitable development opportunities for those involved in the changes. We will encourage our managers to regard each work assignment as offering potential for self-development.
- *Planned development and corporate support*: We will work jointly with individual managers to meet the career options open to them and plan the associated programmes of functional and management development.

Substitute the word 'employee' for 'manager' throughout, and we have a snapshot of the development policy of the surviving organisations of the year 2000. How many will achieve it? Not too many, judging by the rate of progress so far. In a report commissioned by the Manpower Services Commission (as it then was) Alan Mumford and colleagues investigated the careers of 144 directors of more than 40 blue-chip UK organisations.[15] These individuals claimed that their learning had been incidental and accidental, and had occurred as a result of unstructured experiences. Few had any specified career objectives. On the other hand, as Andrew Kakabadse and Charles Margerison found in their research on over 700 US chief executive officers, integrated career experience was what they said was needed for top management.[16]

The Price Waterhouse–Cranfield Survey of five European countries showed that the category of staff receiving the highest increase of investment in training over the last three years in the UK was managers.[17] Interestingly, in Germany and Spain it was professional and technical staff. For four of the five countries, including the UK, manual workers was the category where there was the lowest increase. However, at least there *was* an increase overall. In terms of the origins of the training, line manager requests, closely followed by employee requests and performance appraisal, were the most common sources in the UK. Analysis of business plans and training audits were some way behind as methods of analysing training needs. The most common areas of managerial training were in performance appraisal, staff communication, motivation and team building. The most frequently cited training needs for the future in the UK were, in order:

- people management;
- computers and new technology;
- management of change;
- customer service skills;
- business administration and strategy.

Three of the remaining four countries also cited people management most frequently.

So how far along the development route are we? Two authoritative articles have tried to plot the route – to mark the stages of the development of development. John Burgoyne distinguishes six stages, very reminiscent of the stages of HR strategy development on pp. 93–4. Philip Sadler and Kevin Barham distinguish only three stages.[18] Their third stage, and Burgoyne's fifth and sixth, represent what many organisations' development policies and practices will be like in the year 2000. For the sake of clarity, we'll consider Sadler and Barham's three stages: the fragmented, formalised and focused approaches to training and development.

The *fragmented* approach thinks training is:

- a cost rather than an investment;
- unconnected with organisational goals;
- a luxury;
- directive in style;

- conducted by the training department;
- knowledge based;
- not about development.

The *formalised* approach thinks training is:

- systematic and part of career development;
- limited to HR needs;
- linked to individual needs via appraisal;
- knowledge-based *and* skill oriented;
- linked to career development;
- conducted by trainers *and* line management;
- linked to the job by pre- and post-training work.

The formalised approach fits neatly into the human resource cycle depicted on p. 89. It is the stage at which most external providers of training operate.

Finally, the *focused* approach thinks training and development is:

- a continuous process of learning;
- essential for business survival;
- providing a competitive edge;
- linked both to organisational strategy *and* to individual goals;
- on-the-job plus specialist courses;
- self-selected;
- novel methods of learning;
- the responsibility of the individual's line manager;
- tolerant of a variety of objectives and individual differences.

So the developmental policies of the future won't require the fragmented bolting on of bits of competence to the creaking and groaning structure of the already overburdened manager. They won't involve subject- or discipline-based general management courses, for which Alan Warner lambasts many of the business schools and management centres.[19] They will mean helping people learn from the problems and issues they are currently facing at work. They will mean that all the people in the organisation are concerned with solving the problem, not just those entitled 'managers'. And they will concentrate on the development of teams as much as on the development of individuals.

Toby Wall of the Social and Applied Psychology Unit at Sheffield University relates the following intervention by himself and his colleagues.[20] A lot of output was being lost in a computer-aided manufacturing system in a local organisation. This was due to fairly frequent and lengthy periods of down-time while faults were remedied by engineers. Wall recommended that the operatives themselves should be allowed to remedy the faults. As a result, the length of down-times was reduced: engineers didn't have to be summoned and make their way over to the line. But more important: the operatives learned what caused the faults as a result of repairing them. Consequently they used the system more effectively because they understood it better. The number as well as the length of down-times decreased, and the efficiency increase could be quantified in increased output. People learned on the job, given the opportunity to do so. More and more training and development will consist of organisational interventions which help people solve their problems and help them understand how they've done so. They will be learning to learn.

Self-development

Sadler and Barham's 'focused' stage, and the Management Charter both refer to self-development as the key to the development practice of the future. What exactly is meant by this phrase? George Delf and Bryan Smith define it as

> the process by which individuals:
> - identify their personal development goals
> - consciously take responsibility for planning and taking appropriate action to reach these goals
> - develop and use methods of monitoring progress and assess outcomes
> - re-assess goals in the light of new experiences (and, we may add, of new understanding of our past experiences).
> Self-development differs from traditional approaches to training and development in that it is conceived, planned, controlled and assessed by the individual in his own terms; not those of the trainer, adviser or of the organisation in which he works.[21]

These writers are not talking about individual licence to ask for the content and form of development they wish (although Ford UK has done just that, with the result that the company paid for an employee to learn to become a better tap-dancer). Rather, Delf and Smith refer to the organisation contracting with the employee: employees may have different development needs at different stages of their career, and organisations may view helping them to meet these needs as adding value. In his editorial introduction for *Industrial and Commercial Training* Bryan Smith makes it clear that there is a two-way responsibility: 'Individuals will need to create and use self-development opportunities as an integral element in their organisation's development.'[22]

Given that people differ markedly in how they prefer to learn, and given that we don't know clearly what the jobs of the future will be like and what skills they will need, self-development will win out. Further, as Charles Jackson notes, self-development will be of *all* employees rather than of a group of fast-track stars.[23] People can develop themselves at any time of their lives and from any level. Self-development doesn't mean doing it without help – the organisation supports with resources, time, information, counselling. Nor does it mean doing it in isolation – self-helpers are notorious for getting together in groups. In fact, helping others to develop themselves is a major source of self-development for oneself. What this approach does is to express in action the first of the four balancing acts. It exemplifies the values of development of people and organisational support for them. And it meets our meta-value requirement of being contractual in nature.

What will be the actual mechanisms for self-development? Here are a few, together with some organisations which are already putting them into practice:

– *Development centres*: assessment centres where individuals are given the results to use to guide their self-development (Digital Equipment Corporation; Royal Mail).
– *Degree qualifications, for example MBAs*: either open or tailored to an organisation or a group of organisations (W.H. Smith, Tesco, Burton, Marks & Spencer).
– *Open learning facilities*: usually set up by the organisation; these involve a multi-media approach; computer-based training, interactive video and other methods allow people to work privately, at their own pace, and when it suits them (Guinness).
– *Self-development credits*: all employees are given credits, which they may spend on any form of self-development they wish (Ford UK).
– *Self-development contracts*: individuals agree with their line managers a sequence of self-development activities, which the line manager agrees to support. The annual appraisal interview may be a springboard for such contracts, provided it is not overburdened with too many other purposes as well (BP, BT).

Career management

When you ask people how they have learned what they now know, the overwhelming response is this: they learn most from the sequence of jobs they have done, and from specific problems they have met within them. Their career (in the traditional sense of the sequence of jobs they have held) has developed them. We look now at how jobs and the transitions between them will be handled in the year 2000; we look, in other words, at the organisation's responsibilities for career management. Surviving organisations of the year 2000 won't be those which have given total responsibility for their own developmental direction to individuals. They would have failed to survive if they had. Nor will they be those who sought to develop individuals by fast-track schemes for positions and responsibilities they may not themselves have wanted. Development by the organisation without reference to the individual, and development by the individual without reference to the organisation, are both dead ends.

Nowhere is this clearer than in the case of movement between jobs within organisations. The organisation perceives job moves as:

- a way of getting the right people in the right positions to best achieve its objectives;
- developing them through a sequence of jobs so that they learn from a variety of experience.

Much has been made in recent discussions of the frequent incompatibility of these two aims. The best person for doing the job isn't necessarily the one who will learn most from it. But the real issue is that of the psychological contract. What sort of career development will meet the needs and the expectations of both the individual and the organisation?

It is not hard to see the sort of mechanism required. As John Burgoyne puts it, 'Collaborative career planning is a managed process of dialogue between every manager and the organisation about career prospects and aspirations, skills and development needs' (why just managers?).[24] But it's much harder to put such a process into the overall organisational context. What will career structures in survivor organisations look like, and how will careers be managed? A superb account of best practice for large organisations has recently been provided by Andrew Mayo of ICL.[25]

First let's examine the assumption that people develop as a consequence of the variety of positions they have held. When you ask senior people in organisations what they've learned most from, they nearly all say that a variety of work experiences helped them develop the most.[26] But examined in more detail, these experiences don't necessarily involve a change of job.[27] Almost 200 US executives in their forties were asked for the experiences in their working lives which had made fundamental changes in the way they managed.

- Some were experiences gained on central corporate projects.
- Others involved being entirely responsible for new products, plants or businesses.
- Others again required turning a business around.
- Some involved a sudden quantum leap in the level of responsibility undertaken.

The key experiences typically involved developing new skills, or exercising skills these executives didn't know they possessed. Many managers were allowed to undertake such projects by bosses who were prepared to trust them with difficult assignments, but to take the blame if things went wrong. Careful planning of work experiences within the tenure of a position rather than rapid transfers from job to job may achieve developmental aims just as well. So the definition of careers as a sequence of jobs takes another body blow.

However, the current model operated by several large and successful UK organisations emphasises the developmental advantages to be obtained from career planning. Such organisations are noted for their HR practices, and twelve of them were recently investigated by Wendy Hirsh.[28] Six of the twelve were operating a 'planned development' approach. That is, they sought to develop a group of identified individuals for a target layer of senior jobs. This was generally managed by means of a fast-track scheme, whereby a slice of people was identified as having the potential for senior management. These high fliers were then developed through a varied series of brief jobs, usually involving cross-functional and cross-business moves, and often requiring service abroad. A prime concern of such schemes is that there should always be sufficient qualified people to move up to senior management when needed. Nevertheless, only some senior managers were appointed from the fast track; others had climbed up the hard way. The career of the high fliers was usually managed corporately, although there were moves to devolve to operating units for the younger ones.

Underlying the career management of high fliers is the assumption that people need to move fast across a wide range of jobs in order to have the necessary experience of management ready for promotion at a certain age. However, Hirsh's sample were not clear about what exactly was learned from particular job experiences. They cited:

- functional, business and environmental knowledge;
- managing different sorts of people in different managerial roles;
- gaining confidence and adaptability;

- learning from excellent bosses.

But these were general benefits. Organisations were unwilling to say what was gained from particular sorts of job posting. They seemed to feel that it is beneficial to give high-potential people more experience of wider variety. 'Given the practical problems of finding job opportunities for development, there is little fine tuning at present of learning objectives', says Hirsh charitably.

Hirsh explicitly tells us that these organisations were selected because they had a long history of succession planning and a high profile in this area. As she says, they are not representative even of major UK employers. Lynda Gratton and Michel Syrett make this point forcefully.[29] They note that while such complex and elegant systems are typical of Shell or IBM, they certainly don't meet the needs of other differently structured, but still large and successful, organisations. Comparing IBM with Amstrad, BAT and Hanson, there were huge differences in career development systems. At BAT, for example, different businesses within the company have very different career management systems depending on whether they are start-up or mature, and so on. From the corporate centre, however, a direct interest is taken in those with high potential. In Hanson, on the other hand, there are no corporate HR specialists. The control exercised is financial, and career management systems are left to businesses and are not monitored corporately.

Of course we can allocate these four organisations to the strategic types of chapter 6. IBM is an archetypal analyser academy, for example, while Hanson is a prospector baseball team. Gratton and Syrett's findings support our hypotheses about the internal and external labour markets of each. But the research evidence tells us that even this is far too simplified and Anglo-centric an analysis. Paul Evans compared the fast-track high-flier career systems of UK analyser academies with German and Japanese organisations.[30] He found that top German firms such as Bayer, Hoechst, Siemens, Volkswagen and BASF treat their graduate entrants very differently from UK firms. During an initial period of up to two years they will move rapidly from function to function in order to establish where their talents lie. Then they will often remain within a single functional career structure for the rest of their working lives, although this pattern is beginning to break down. There is now some interfunctional movement at middle management level. Nevertheless, the two-yearly cross-functional job move for young managers certainly isn't part of the German pattern.

Nor is it part of the Japanese system. There one enters a technical or an administrative career path, depending on the subject of one's degree. These paths rarely intersect, and specialists are more likely to achieve senior status than are others. The first seven or eight years on the administrative path are a trial period with much rotation among departments and much training. Employees are assessed seven or eight times a year. They then move in their early thirties into real managerial responsibility, and stay at least four years in each job. On the other hand, spending much longer than four years in a job is an indication that they will not reach senior management. Obviously the Japanese model requires extremely careful preparation of an elite to do real jobs in the organisation (you can't escape the need to implement your plans and answer for their results in a 4–5 year stint).

The idea that there is one single form of career system in operation in each organisation is also likely to be an oversimplification. There *may* be a single career system for upper middle and senior management. But as James Baron and colleagues demonstrated in a huge and meticulous study of 1,883 jobs in 100 Californian organisations, there are likely to be several different job ladders with little or no connections between them in a single operation.[31] Baron found that

– jobs requiring firm-specific training were more likely to be in promotion ladders;
– professional and technical jobs were less likely to be in promotion ladders than line management jobs in manufacturing industry;
– transfer from one ladder to another was possible: for men (but not for women) in production-related administrative jobs, who moved to junior management, and for people in individual organisations where there was open job advertisement or managed cross-functional transfer for development purposes;
– of 268 promotion ladders investigated 191 were occupied exclusively by men, 17 exclusively by women, and 60 were mixed.

Admittedly, these results were obtained in the 1970s. But the number of different career ladders within organisations often unconnected to each other and differentiated by gender, is incredible. It shows how the development of *all* of the individuals in an organisation to their full potential is likely to be frustrated by rigid career paths. How often are female secretarial staff promoted to management?[32] How often are technical specialists members of boards of directors? How frequently do people who have actually served customers take positions in the corporate planning function?

Fast-track schemes tend to perpetuate these self-contained career ladders. They buy for a few a richly varied sequence of cross-functional moves, but they can bring with them a host of harmful consequences, as many writers have noted.[33]

- They demotivate the rest of the employees – the second-class citizen syndrome.
- They usually rely on early and unreliable assessments of long-term potential – people develop at different ages.
- The jobs held are often 'developmental' rather than 'real' jobs.
- High fliers seek to impress and make their mark in each job by introducing change.
- However, they do not remain in the job long enough to implement this change or to be held responsible for its consequences.
- They fail to obtain a solid grounding in any one specialism – the cult of the generalist amateur lingers on.
- They are selected by senior people who choose in their own image – appropriate for the present but it's not going to fit the future.
- Selection for the fast track is a self-fulfilling prophecy – 'these people are high fliers so they must be good'.
- High fliers have inflated expectations for their career advancement which often can't be met – they may leave as a consequence.

But it is not so much these unintended consequences which will result in the demise of such career systems before long; it's their unsuitability to the context of the 90s. Internal labour markets are breaking down. Corporate control of careers is being devolved. Layers of management are being removed. New jobs are continuously being created. New sorts of people are entering management at different ages. Matching people to jobs for the future won't be on: the people won't be staying, and the jobs won't be in existence. Development will be much shorter term: it will be between projects and assignments more than between jobs. It will be negotiated between individuals and their bosses rather than determined by means of secret assessments of potential. And it will be organisation-wide rather than limited to a few 'heirs apparent'. By these means the key values of development of people *and* supportive teamwork to aid responsiveness to change and risk and innovation will be expressed. The achievement of our first balancing act, between change and support, will be promoted.

Managing transitions

Development through jobs and projects, moreover, has its costs. Some of the transitions are very radical. More than 50 per cent of Nicholson and West's sample had changed function in their last job move.[34] So frequent were these managers' moves that, Nicholson and West argue, they had no period of stability in a job. No sooner had they adapted themselves to a new job and the new job to themselves than they were preparing for the next one. There was little opportunity for the reflection upon experience which is likely to be as important for learning as the experience itself.

Nicholson and West have provided a clear picture of the sorts of transition UK managers make, and the different phases of these transitions (see Table 7.1). They note that transitions may involve leaving the organisation or staying (stay or leave); promotion or not (up, same or down); and changing function or not (across or within). Any transition will involve one, two or three of these changes. In order of frequency (per cent) the eight most frequent types of transition were as follows:

Table 7.1 *Types and phases of transitions made by UK managers*

Type	Organisation		Level		Function		Frequency
1	Stay	+	Up	+	Across	=	27.6
2	Leave	+	Up	+	Across	=	24.6
3	Stay	+	Same	+	Across	=	10.0
4	Stay	+	Up	+	Within	=	8.4
5	Leave	+	Up	+	Within	=	8.3
6	Leave	+	Same	+	Across	=	6.9
7	Leave	+	Down	+	Across	=	5.0
8	Leave	+	Same	+	Within	=	4.3

Source: Nicholson and West (1988) *Managerial Job Change.* Cambridge: Cambridge University Press

To make these results more real, consider the following examples of the three most frequent transition types:

- a leader of an audit team of 3 who becomes manager of the internal IT services (stay up across);
- the manager of R&D in a Ministry of Defence establishment who leaves to be Chief Executive of a small consultancy (leave up across);
- a supervisor of secretarial staff who becomes supervisor of salespersons (stay same across).

So by far the majority changed their function, and nearly half left the organisation. More than half indicated that the job to which they moved was a newly created one, and the average length of time in a job was three years. A picture of rapid and radical change! Perhaps these 2000-plus members of the British Institute of Management didn't include many specialists, who tend to belong to their professional associations. Nevertheless, the data are still amazing.

When contrasting their present with their previous jobs, respondents quoted three separate areas of experience. First, the novelty of the new job – differences in tasks, skills and methods. Not surprisingly, this tended to be most noticeable to those who changed functions and organisations. Second came the learning requirement (the need to develop major new skills), and third the opportunity to use previously acquired skills. So they're faced with a daunting prospect indeed.

It's hardly surprising that people find particular parts of the transition difficult. They are somewhat anxious during the preparation phase, while they're still in the old job. What causes them most worry is how well they'll perform, and whether their contributions will be valued by important people. Women have more anxiety at this stage than men – they often have the additional problem of gaining acceptance in masculine environments.

When encountering the new job, people are disappointed with the training provided, and especially with the quality of communications and decision-making; inefficiency and autocracy go hand in hand. Low-profile supervision by their new boss tends to be interpreted as neglect. Overall, they are surprised at these shortcomings – their expectations are unfulfilled.

These findings about the difficulties involved in transitions are in marked contrast to Nicholson and West's findings regarding the longer-term benefits of job change. These were in the main highly positive. As they say, 'People tend to move out of jobs where they feel there is restricted scope for growth, and tend to reap benefits of improved work characteristics in their new roles.' So transition management must be a key concern for organisations in the future.

So instead of 'selling' the job by raising unrealistic expectations, or making wholesale structural changes and expecting to be able to insert employees into the new slots, the survivors of the year 2000 will be using some or all of the following systems:

– career audits: ways of discovering what shorter-term moves employees expect, and how these differ from what the organisation thought they expected and from what it expects of them;
– information systems about general HR directions and specific

internal vacancies; and ways in which these may relate to experience and skill requirements;[35]
- career counselling in which information and knowledge about their own career anchors and expectations may be acquired;
- career interviews, at which individual and organisational expectations may be negotiated with one's line managers;
- the opportunity to shadow or at least question the present job-holder; some degree of overlap in time;
- the provision of a mentor in the new job to aid the transition, put the newcomer in contact with the network, and so on;
- the management of relocation to ensure satisfactory adjustments for partner and family.[36]

But career structures and career transitions are areas of acute concern for the next ten years. The internal labour markets are crumbling and insecurity of employment is increasing. Jobs are considered important, but the transition process between them is largely ignored. The achievement of our first balance – between change and support – will be hard indeed. It will be even harder if some of the currently fashionable solutions are retained. Generic managerial competencies, fast-track schemes, piecemeal discipline-based training – all these are tools of the past rather than the future. They match neither organisational nor individual needs, let alone striking an appropriate and negotiated balance between them. The future will see organisations which succeed engaging in:

- development and training on the job and usually in teams;
- development of all employees, not just those called managers;
- negotiated career development;
- management of transitions.

Some final questions

About your own career
- Which personal competencies do you feel you need to develop for the future? On what basis have you identified them?
- What specific plans do you have for meeting your development needs?
- What specifically developmental activities have you undertaken hitherto? Which party played the greater part in deciding on them – you or the organisation? How, exactly, were these decisions arrived at?
- Do you know what your next job will be in your organisation? How different do you think it will be from your present job? How well prepared will you be for it?

About your organisation

- Does your organisation analyse jobs in terms of the competencies they require? To what uses does it put this analysis – for performance appraisal? assessment of development needs? assessment of potential? succession planning? recruitment and selection?

- Which of the three stages of training and development activity has your organisation reached: fragmented, formalised or focused (see pp. 108–9)? What are the main reasons why it is at this stage and not another? Or is it in between stages? What is pushing it?

- Does your organisation use job postings for developmental purposes? For whom, and at what stage of their organisational careers?

- How does your organisation manage the careers of functional specialists – or doesn't it manage careers at all?

Notes

1 H. Mintzberg (1973) *The Nature of Managerial Work*. New York: Harper & Row; R. Stewart (1985) *The Reality of Management*, 2nd edn. London: Pan Books.

2 J. Greatrex and P. Phillips (1989) 'Oiling the wheels of competence', *Personnel Management*, 21 (8): 36–9.

3 R.E. Boyatzis (1982) *The Competent Manager: a Model for Effective Performance*. New York: John Wiley; H.M. Schroder (1989) *Managerial Competence: the Key to Excellence*. Iowa: Kendall Hunt.

4 M. Day (1988) 'Managerial competence and the charter initiative', *Personnel Management*, 20 (8): 30–4.

5 Ibid., p. 31.

6 W. Hirsh and S. Bevan (1988) *What Makes a Manager? In Search of a Language for Management Skills*. Brighton: Institute of Manpower Studies.

7 American Management Association (1988) *Regulations*.

8 C. Handy (1987) *The Making of Managers*. London: Manpower Services Commission, National Economic Development Council and Confederation of British Industry; J. Constable and R. McCormick (1987) *The Making of British Managers*, London: British Institute of Management and Confederation of British Industry.

9 T. Glaze (1989) 'Cadbury's dictionary of competence', *Personnel Management*, 21 (7): 44–8.

10 Ibid., my emphasis.

11 Greatrex and Phillips, op. cit.

12 T. Cockerill (1989) 'The kind of competence for rapid change', *Personnel Management*, 21 (9): 52–8.

13 Schroder, op. cit.

14 G. Prentice (1990) 'Adapting management style for the organisation of the future', *Personnel Management*, 22 (6): 58–62.

15 A. Mumford, G. Robinson and D. Stradling (1989) *Developing Directors*. London: Training Agency/IMCB.

16 A. Kakabadse and C. Margerison (1988) 'Top executives: addressing their management development needs', *Leadership and Organisation Development Journal*, 9 (4): 17–21.

17 *The Price Waterhouse Cranfield Project Report* (1990). London: Price Waterhouse.

18 J. Burgoyne (1988) 'Management development for the individual *and* the organisation', *Personnel Management*, 20 (6): 40–4; P. Sadler and K. Barham (1988) 'From Franks to the future', *Personnel Management*, 20 (5): 48–51.

19 A. Warner (1990) 'Where business schools fail to meet business needs', *Personnel Management*, 22 (7): 52–8.

20 T. Wall (1990) Personal communication.

21 G. Delf and T.B. Smith (1978) Strategies for promoting self development', *Industrial and Commercial Training*, 10: 494–501.

22 T.B. Smith (1990) Editorial comment, in *Industrial and Commercial Training*, 22: 17–19.

23 C. Jackson (1990) *Careers Counselling in Organisations: the Way Forward*. Brighton: Institute of Manpower Studies.

24 Burgoyne, op. cit., p. 43.

25 A. Mayo (1991) *Managing Careers*. London: Institute of Personnel Management.

26 A. Kakabadse and C. Margerison, op. cit.

27 M. McCall, M. Lombardo and A. Morrison (1989) 'Great leaps in career development', *Across the Board*, March 88–90.

28 W. Hirsh (1990) *Succession Planning: Current Practice and Future Issues*. Brighton: Institute of Manpower Studies.

29 L. Gratton and M. Syrett (1990) 'Heirs apparent: succession strategies for the future', *Personnel Management*, 22 (1): 34–8.

30 P. Evans (1990) 'International management development and the balance between generalism and professionalism', *Personnel Management*, 22 (12): 46–50.

31 J.N. Baron, A. Davis-Blake and W.T. Bielby (1986) 'The structure of opportunity: how promotion ladders vary within and among organisations', *Administrative Science Quarterly*, 31: 248–73.

32 P. Cole and M. Povall (1991) 'Take a new career path, Ms. Jones', *Personnel Management*, 23 (5): 45–7.

33 Hirsh, op. cit.; P.H. Thompson, K.L. Kirkham and J. Dixon (1985) 'Warning: The fast track may be hazardous to organisational health', *Organisational Dynamics*, Spring: 21–33; B.E. Kovach (1987) 'The derailment of fast-track managers', *Organisational Dynamics*, Summer: 41–8.

34 N. Nicholson and M. West (1988) *Managerial Job Change: Men and Women in Transition*. Cambridge: Cambridge University Press.

35 A. Mayo (1990) 'Linking manpower planning and management development', *Industrial and Commercial Training*, 22 (3): 3–12.

36 N. Forster and T. Munton (1991) 'The danger of a false move', *Personnel Management*, 23 (1): 40–3.

8

Loyalty and Respect

Scotty's gripes

The Sunday Times recently carried a story about executive leasing.[1] Executive leasing is a scheme whereby experienced managers are leased to organisations for a period normally of between three and nine months. They are not consultants, for they report to the board of the company to whom they are leased, and carry full executive authority. They carry out assignments such as turning round an ailing subsidiary, integrating a newly acquired business into the organisation, or filling in the position of a senior manager who has left unexpectedly. Approximately twenty leasing companies now exist in the UK making a good living out of hiring out executives. There are no shortage of resources: one such company has had 10,000 applications to be placed on the executive register. Another received 800 even before it went public. Senior managers obviously want out of organisations.

Lower down the hierarchy, the downward spiral in employee morale also continues.[2] Employees:

- have less confidence in management than they had in 1987;
- are less convinced about job security than they were in 1987;
- are not so inclined to identify with company goals as they were in 1987.

Indeed, as far as identification with the company goals is concerned, levels have fallen back to those demonstrated in 1977.

So there is a great deal of dissatisfaction around. According to *The Sunday Times*, this has transmitted itself to those employees aged between 25 and 30 who either have an MBA or expect to get one shortly. Only 20 per cent of a sample of 200 of these young aspirants wanted to pursue a lifetime corporate career.

Why should present and future executives be turned off in this way? One plausible reason is that they don't feel that our second balance has been satisfactorily achieved. They don't think that the loyalty and commitment package that's expected of them is balanced by the same degree of attention on the organisation's part to their own individual rights and needs. It's worth looking in more detail at what loyalty and commitment actually bring these days.

Many employees, and especially middle managers, have served their organisation well. They have changed function more than once, surrendering the option of developing and retaining specific functional expertise. They have usually done this because they've been asked, not because they see cross-functional experience as the fast route to the top. They've built up their knowledge of their organisation over time, so they know how to get things done. People go to them for help – to get a route map, to find out the right person to contact, to learn what the pitfalls are for the unwary. They are the repository of the organisational culture, which is a major factor in keeping the place going. Organisational survival is, after all, the outcome of a delicate balance between maintenance and adaptation.

As they stayed longer, they gained more and more organisation-specific knowledge, but became less and less knowledgeable in any one know-how area. Consequently, they are less employable elsewhere. Along came the delayering and the slimming down of the 80s, and the outcome was inevitable. They were told they were now no longer the essential and reliable bedrock of the organisation that they thought they were. So like the honourable English gentlemen that they are, they make the ultimate sacrifice, softened marginally by generous redundancy terms. Scotty has been transformed into Captain Oates overnight. Or they remained but were expected to double their workload because there were fewer of them than there used to be. What's more, any lingering hope of further promotion is taken away, since delayering has removed entire levels of the career structure. Such are the rewards for loyalty!

Get out and chance the job market, or stay in at the same level and double your workload: not much of a career option in this dilemma! But that's not all; insult has been piled upon injury: having got used to the idea that they aren't high fliers on the fast track, the Scotties of the organisational world have even lost the tag of solid citizen.[3] In a piece of poorly researched and opportunistic writing they have been branded as deadwood. The so-called 'Peter principle', masquerading as a universal scientific law, asserts that they have been promoted to the level of their incompetence. Otherwise they would have progressed higher, it is implied. What's more, because they have grown old (or at least middle-aged) in the organisation, their loyalty is outweighed by their lack of the golden elixir of youth, a currently overvalued commodity.

Of course, the Peter principle completely ignores the obvious structural reasons for not being further promoted. The normal pyramid shape becomes narrower as you get higher. The tag 'plateaued manager' at least recognises this fact, but still has unfortunate connotations. For by using the mountain metaphor it implies that everyone wants to reach the summit but that many are disappointed in this aim. As John Veiga has found,[4] 'deadwood' plateaued managers (poor performers stuck at a particular level) tend to have moved earlier in their career between other organisations. The good performers ('solid citizens') are the ones who have loyally stayed, regardless of the absence of promotional opportunities.

Current strategic movements add to Scotty's discomfort. As John Slocum and colleagues point out, *defender* organisations are likely to offer more opportunity for advancement to production and finance people.[5] This is the strategic type where cost control and product quality and reliability are crucial; production and finance functions are therefore visible, valued and promoted. But in the UK we have seen a move away from the *defender* to the *analyser* and *prospector* strategic types (see Figure 6.1, p. 83). These need sales, marketing and design people; opportunities for the productive core and the financial controllers are reduced. Just those stalwarts who did the basic and crucial jobs see themselves overtaken by 'smart young things on the periphery'. Moreover, the move from one strategic type to another is fraught with peril. Sudden lurches into *reactor* mode occur, where redundancies are likely until progress towards another mode can be resumed.

So the solid citizens of the organisational world have had a lot to put up with in the last ten years, and there's no sign of the speed of strategic shifts easing off. Labour markets will become more external, as stars are brought in at all levels. More layers will be stripped out in more organisations, so that the pyramid turns into a suburban semi. Increased technical sophistication will make it harder and harder to go back to one's original specialisation or to acquire a new one. Mergers and alliances will mean new cultures to understand and more threats of redundancy.

So past experience and future prospects look grim for Scotty. He's kept his side of the bargain, but much good has it done him. He doesn't believe the organisation has reciprocated; only by explicitly recognising his rights can it make amends.

According to a recent survey of over 3,000 managers aged between 40 and 55, with an average length of service of seventeen years,[6] the main gripes are:

- lack of development opportunities: 45 per cent had experienced no formal training and development in the last five years;

- inflexibility of benefits: they want shares, better pensions, more holidays and fewer hours;
- inflexibility of retirement process: they want part-time work, and so on;
- pay ceilings and promotion barriers for people their age.

They see themselves, realistically or not, as having all sorts of potential roles to play:

- internal consultant managing projects;
- mentor;
- managing interfaces within and outside the organisation;
- managing spin-offs, joint ventures and alliances.

Organisational policies are clearly at odds with these expectations. For example, in 1990 increases in total compensation were significantly lower than the rise in basic salary, showing that changes in the non-cash elements haven't kept pace with cash rises.[7] So much for flexibility of reward systems, one of the gripes of our loyal Scotties. Where there is some flexibility, it's very limited. For example, a hospital trust will allow managers to choose between superannuation, car leasing or cash to the value of 10 per cent of salary.[8] That's just one specific area in which loyal employees' expectations aren't at present met.

Manipulation or contract?

So what underlies Scotty's past sufferings and present gripes? And how will the survival organisations of the year 2000 be treating their trusties? The answer lies far deeper than superannuation or car leasing. It involves nothing less than a profound transformation in the relationship between organisation and employee.

In the UK we have always accepted an inequality of power between these two. The clearest evidence of this can be seen from the language that we use about it. I'm not referring here to slogans like 'management's right to manage'. I'm talking about the very language of management itself. We speak of incentives, to pull people towards targets; of rewards, which reinforce their performance; of culture change programmes, aimed at improving their attitudes, values and behaviour. We talk about motivating people, developing them, deploying them and utilising them. In sum, our language is about doing things to people to make them behave in different ways.

Language is used to make sense of and legitimise ambiguous situations.[9] The relationship between employer and employee has always been an ambiguous one, and the party with the greater power has called the linguistic tune. The language of 'scientific' management theory and practice is the tune we have played to throughout the twentieth century. Based on the needs of semi-automated manufacturing industry, it has been softened by the honourable humanitarian paternalism of Cadbury, Rowntree or Pilkington. But essentially it's the tune called by organisations, because they have held the whip hand.

Underpinning the use of managerialist language are various assumptions about which we are becoming more and more suspicious. Underlying the idea of doing things to people so that they change their behaviour are the assumptions that we can talk in terms of simple cause and effect about human behaviour, and that the cause which produces the effect is something we can manipulate.

Here's an example to bring this point home. An organisation observes that many of the managers it would like to retain are leaving, and go on to receive higher salaries from their new employers. It infers that they left their present jobs in order to get a higher salary, so it increases the salary of those who remain, believing that this will keep them loyal. As Stephen Bevan has shown,[10] people have all sorts of reasons for leaving, and the increased salary in the new job is probably a consequence of leaving rather than the motivation for it.

However, we seem stuck with the language of manipulation. We believe that we can change people by doing things to them – that we are engineers of behaviour. In tune with the rationalism of science and technology, we think we can control and predict. Our managerial language is all about *how* this can be done. It seldom queries *why* it should be. When outcomes are as we want them, we can attribute this to what we've done; when they aren't we say our systems aren't developed enough. In private, chief executives often indicate that they haven't the faintest idea why things turned out so well/badly; but this honest expression of ignorance doesn't usually find its way into the public arena.

There is an alternative reality, and an alternative language for describing it. This is the reality I sketched out in chapter 4. The language is the language of *contract*. But just to bring home the message, think back to the 20 per cent quoted at the beginning of this chapter. Only 20 per cent of current prospective MBA graduates want a corporate career. These are people who have deliberately acquired a broad business educational qualification, ideally suiting them to progress towards general management. Yet only one fifth of them expect to use it within the setting of a business organisation. There's something wrong somewhere!

So the reality and the language have to change. The future reality is that of equal power and equal rights of the parties. Equality of power is slowly coming about because know-how is scarce and there will be a seller's labour market in many skills. In addition sellers of know-how labour won't merely have a choice between organisational employers; they will often be able to choose between being organisationally or self-employed. And equality of rights is coming about partly because of developments in employment law and precedent. For example, if an employee has received favourable appraisals, has remained with an organisation for some time, and has been vouchsafed vision and mission statements which express how much the organisation values her, then dismissal can be difficult.[11] Unfortunately for Scotty, though, the Kirks and the Spocks, the risk-takers and the knowledge workers, are likely to have the greater labour market power.

So what is the new reality, and the new assumptions on which it is based? It assumes, first of all, that organisation is a social, collaborative activity rather than a controlling, manipulative one. It recognises that different groups and individuals at present possess different degrees of power, especially during the current recession. But it insists that these inequalities in power make equality of rights all the more important. And it insists on *contract* between parties with equal rights as the essence of the employment relationship. It is the language of contract which will give meaning and legitimation to the reality of the year 2000.

What is implied by the idea of *contract*? As Bruce and Eileen Drake observe, there are four necessary conditions for a satisfactory contract to be made.[11]

The parties must have full knowledge of the terms and conditions

Obviously, neither organisations nor individuals can make very detailed long-term commitments. But one of the conditions of the initial psychological contract should be that it will be renegotiated periodically as needs change. However, this does not prevent some general commitments being made after an initial period; for example an agreement that changes of job within an organisation should be by mutual agreement and without prejudice.

The parties must not misrepresent the situation to each other

Prospective and present employees are currently expected to be truthful about their experience, qualifications and circumstances. But organisations seem to have more licence. They can often exploit people's need to belong and their need to invest their work with meaning. This can be done by propagating a 'one big happy family' mythology, and by pretending that a single prime value or objective informs the whole organisation. In sum, organisations can misrepresent the situation by cynical manipulation of symbols – the 'management of meaning'. They can also, more commonly, put a more favourable gloss on events than they merit. Such misrepresentation has no part in a truly contractual relationship.

Neither party should be under coercion or duress
Individuals can hold organisations to ransom, for example by threatening to leave at a point when this would scupper an ongoing project. But organisations have a wider range of sanctions and controls at their disposal, and they usually have many more resources than individuals or their representatives, for example in terms of access to legal services.

Neither party should be expected to commit an immoral
act as a consequence of the contract
As we saw on pp. 51–2, some organisations have expressed a commitment to this condition in published ethical codes, which recognise the role of individual and corporate citizenship.

Any contract worth the name has the above four features. What the idea of contract expresses is that each of the parties has rights, and that a reciprocal relationship is involved. Reciprocity, after all, is the basis of any social relationship. By the year 2000 we will be recognising that that's what an organisation is: a complex set of social collaborative relations, rather than a machine or a Darwinian species.

Of course we are very Anglocentric if we think the idea of a reciprocal psychological contract is a new one. Apart from being preached by far-sighted transatlantic scholars such as Chris Argyris since the 1960s, it's been enshrined in the German system for years. There they have a right of codetermination, but participation in decisions is matched by shared responsibility for their outcomes. But the main point for Scotty is that mutual expectations can be equitably agreed so that a satisfactory and explicit psychological contract can be made.

Scotty's contract

It's not so easy as it sounds. The surviving organisations of the year 2000 will have recognised what it really is that Scotty is offering, and therefore, what it is that he might reasonably expect them to reciprocate with. One thing is sure – Scotty is offering more than his labour, and he'll be expecting more in return than his wages.

So what *is* his position? Basically, he's suffering opportunity costs. Unlike Mr Spock, who is continually increasing his employability by brushing up his technical know-how to a burnished brilliance, Scotty suffers a *decrease in employability* after a while. By agreeing to change functions to help the organisation, and by acquiring lots of specific organisational knowledge, he's less attractive to other organisations. The longer he stays the older he gets – in itself a handicap in the employment stakes, as witness all the job advertisements which specify a (youthful) age range.

There is a second opportunity cost suffered by Scotty (and usually by the other crew members as well). This is in terms of *other life roles* which have to be surrendered or played inadequately. The roles of parent, spouse or partner are the most obvious; child, friend and citizen roles also clamour for attention. Devotion to the organisation by definition leaves less time and less energy for these other roles.

But Scotty also often surrenders *preferred roles at work*. Career anchors (see pp. 59–60) vary across individuals. Some Scotties with a career anchor of technical and functional competence may have surrendered this value to become a generalist manager at the organisation's request. Others, longing to be creative, find themselves doing essentially conservative jobs, preserving the fabric of the organisation. Others again have always wanted the autonomy and independence to run their own show, but have loyally subjugated these ambitions to corporate directions or been bought off with promises.

In many cases the Scotties of the organisation have surrendered more than other roles they would have preferred. They've also surrendered part of themselves – their identity. The loss of the opportunity to play a role can have this effect – the scientist or engineer whose professional skill formed a major part of their identity; or the parents forced to send their children to a private boarding school as the result of an overseas posting. So can being expected to do things which violate one's view of oneself; selecting subordinates for redundancy, for example. People expect to have to wear a variety of hats, but they know there are some which are simply 'not them'.

Instead of winding up the ratchet to achieve a yet higher level of performance by means of greater effort and more time put into the job, organisations of the year 2000 will be looking at the costs such expectations carry. They will recognise that these costs peak at different points in people's lives; and they will be prepared to minimise them by mutual agreement.

Taking the costs Scotty typically suffers, organisations in the year 2000 will be increasing his employment security as he decreases his employability. They will be renegotiating the psychological contract to suit his preferred career anchor. They will adapt their expectations in accordance with the pressure of other life roles. And they will respect their people's need for personal identity and integrity.

We can expect to see a huge variety of contracts and systems geared to individual needs. For example:

- self-employment;
- part-time;
- fixed-term;
- job share;
- sabbaticals;
- career breaks;
- annual hours;
- flexitime;
- phased retirement;
- secondment;
- subcontracting;
- cafeteria benefits;[12]
- childcare provision;
- paternity leave.

Jobs and families

But to specify the systems of the future without considering the contractual values that underpin them is futile. As Jane Pickard has pointed out,[13] all of these systems *can* be used to achieve the organisational aim of cutting costs while maintaining or improving performance. They may also have the hidden agenda of derecognising the unions. Rather than listing them baldly, it is more illuminating to look at one issue in more detail: how will organisational and family roles mesh in the year 2000? The underlying values will hopefully become clearer.

To look at this issue solely in terms of the care of pre-school children is a grave current danger. Family life isn't just about childcare. It's about:

- what happens to children after school's finished;
- what happens when they are ill;

- who supports them at school events;
- what happens during the school holidays;
- when parents and children can do things together;
- what happens to ageing and ailing grandparents.

To look at the issue in terms of helping women achieve their organisational career aims is likewise mistaken; parents are male and female.

Just to emphasise this point, let's return to Nicholson and West's huge sample of UK managers, the majority of whom were male.[14] When asked what was their central life interest, 50 per cent of the single ones said it was their career, 28 per cent their family. Of those who were married but had no children, the order was reversed – 31 and 63 respectively. And for those married with children, only 23 per cent regarded their career as central, compared with 71 per cent for their family.

Much of our thinking involves tinkering with ideas still based on sex stereotypes. We've come round to the idea that women want careers and that organisations need them; but we're still hooked on the notions that men don't want an equal share in bringing up their children; and that men and women believe that the man's career should come first. We will have to get used to the idea that where there are two parents their careers cannot be considered independently. And where there is one, his or her career will certainly not follow a traditional pattern but may nevertheless be highly productive. Families, not employees, are stakeholders in the future organisations.

This is not to urge organisations on to a pro-family campaign. It is equally important to recognise the needs of non-parents and non-couples, and to contract with them in mutually acceptable ways. What *is* implied, though, is a redefinition of success and of what it takes. Two-thirds of senior executives in the USA who are female are also childless; not many of the males are. Is being a senior executive incompatible with being a mother? Or do we expect the abnegation of the role of mother *en route* to the top? Success will be seen more and more as integrating work and family life at whatever level of the organisation one finishes up. But organisations will be missing out if they don't make such integration possible for senior executives, for they will be fishing for leaders in an ever-decreasing pool of those willing to sacrifice their all. Anyway, is the willingness to work intensely hard all one's life a suitable criterion for selecting senior executives?

The problems of coping with family life when only one parent, the man, is a manager have been explored by Paul Evans and

Fernando Bartolome.[15] Of these male managers and their wives, 45 per cent characterised the relationship between work and home as a *spillover*. This is especially the case when the manager is struggling to launch his career and establish himself. The next most frequent relationship was *independence*: work and home seem to exist side by side. *Conflict* between home and work such that they could not easily be reconciled came next in order of frequency. So, clearly, work impinges on home life for a large number of male managers. It often takes a crisis for them to stop construing their home life as a prop and support to their working life, and their level of work commitment as being necessary to support their family. When such family crises do not force a re-evaluation, the danger is of overinvolvement in an exciting career (Kirk) or self-sacrifice in a plateaued one (Scotty).

Dual careers

But this research doesn't raise the more fundamental issues of the 90s. How are we to think about dual careers, given that most couples will both expect a career; and that both partners will expect equity with the other in career development opportunities?

The traditional way of dealing with dual careers when the couple has children has been what Una Sekaran and Douglas Hall have called the *sequential* pattern.[16] The man carries on his career as usual, helping (hopefully) where he can. The woman

- works, then beings up a family;
- works, has a family, and returns to work; or
- has a family, then works.

When we look at *simultaneous* careers, a different pattern emerges.

- Both man and woman develop their careers before they have children. The adjustments they have to make to fit in with each other's career are relatively minor (e.g. same geographical area).
- In their later twenties or early thirties they have children. The combination of the need to establish their careers firmly and the demanding role of parents is overwhelming. Typically, the woman surrenders more of her career than does the man. This is easier for her – it fits in with organisational and social norms ('paternity leave, whatever next?'). But there are other potential criteria for deciding who slows down their career more (or whether they both do to an equal extent):
    Who's earning more?

Whose career has more of a timetable?

Who's more committed to work?

- The children are at school. There is still a major parenting role to play, but more time and effort can be devoted by parents to their career. If the woman has taken the major parenting role at the previous stage, then she has some career catching up to do. The man, meanwhile, will be trying to catch up with his children: 'I hardly know them as people.'
- The children have left home. The woman, if she has undertaken the major parenting role, is likely to be in mid-career and cherishing her independence. The man is plateaued, and realising that there are other important things in life besides his work.

Sekaran and Hall suggest that the man's and woman's careers tend to get out of synch with each other in this scenario. One or the other may miss out on the organisational timetable when the children are young, if one takes on the major parent role. So the organisation's expectations may be upset, *and* the couple may grow apart, failing to have shared experiences.

The survivor organisations of the year 2000 will think in terms of *couple careers* as well as individual careers. They will relax early career timetables so that both men and women can periodically ease off during young childhood *and* during schooldays. They will provide later career development opportunities, allowing men to avoid the early burnout syndrome, women to overcome the re-entry difficulties caused by the current prevalent pattern. Organisations will be doing this not out of concern for the family or to help keep relationships intact. They will be doing it because it is part of the contract they must negotiate in order to attract and retain the staff they need; it will bring them corporate advantage.

As for the couples, all sorts of benefits accrue from dual careers.[17] For the man:

- another income means he is less dependent on the organisation, and so has greater bargaining power;
- success and satisfaction can be derived from doing a good job rather than climbing a ladder;
- support, ideas and counsel can come from a partner at a similar stage in her career.

For the couple:

- their relationship is more central;
- their financial security is greater;
- they can take risks;

- the family versus work conflict is reduced;
- the children have working role models of both sexes.

But for the woman, the following costs will accrue unless values change:

- still not being taken seriously at work;
- still acting as household manager and social secretary;
- feelings of guilt and need to be superwoman.

What is certain is that the issue of dual careers and of families will be high on the agenda when the psychological contract is negotiated in the year 2000. It will be there not because organisations believe that they can get more work out of people for less money, but because surviving organisations will be treating employees as equals with whom one negotiates rather than as resources one manipulates.

Some final questions

About your own career

- How long have you been in your present organisation? Are you presently more employable elsewhere than when you joined it, or less employable? Why?
- How does your organisation currently benefit from your experience within it? How could it benefit?
- Which of your preferred work roles have you surrendered or foregone at the organisation's request?
- Which of your other life roles have suffered as a result of your organisational role?
- Are you part of a dual-career couple? If so, how has this affected your career? How has it affected your partner's? Are you male or female? What difference has your gender made?

About your organisation

- How does your organisation recognise and reward loyalty and long service?
- If there have been redundancies of long-serving employees, how have these been handled? What aspects of a psychological contract were broken?
- In what ways if any does your organisation recognise that you have a life outside the organisation?
- How flexible is it in its employment contracts? How could it become more flexible?

Notes

1 T. Lunn (1991) 'Restive executives find escape route', *The Sunday Times*, 13 January.

2 A. Arkin (1990) 'Downward spiral in employee morale looks set to continue', *Personnel Management Plus*, November: 3.

3 T.P. Ference, J.A.F. Stoner and E.K. Warren (1977) 'Managing the career plateau', *Academy of Management Review*, October: 602–12.

4 J.F. Veiga (1981) 'Plateaued versus nonplateaued managers: career patterns, attitudes, and path potential', *Academy of Management Journal*, 24: 566–78.

5 J.W. Slocum, W.L. Cron, R.W. Hansen and S. Rawlings (1985) 'Business strategy and the management of plateaued employees', *Academy of Management Journal*, 28: 133–54.

6 J. Lewis and C. Mcaverty (1991) 'Facing up to the needs of the older manager', *Personnel Management*, 23 (1): 32–5.

7 A. Arkin (1991) 'Cafeteria benefits trend grows', *Personnel Management Plus*, March: 7.

8 P. Hilton (1991) 'Hospital trusts aim for cafeteria pay', *Personnel Management Plus*, February: 1.

9 J. Pfeffer (1981) 'Management as symbolic action', in L.L. Cummings and B.M. Staw (eds), *Research in Organisational Behaviour*, vol. 3. Greenwich, CT: JAI Press.

10 S. Bevan (1990) *Managing Staff Retention in the 1990s*. Brighton: Institute of Manpower Studies.

11 B.H. Drake and E. Drake (1988) 'Ethical and legal aspects of managing corporate cultures', *Californian Management Review*, Winter: 107–23.

12 C. Woodley (1990) 'The cafeteria route to compensation', *Personnel Management*, 22 (5): 42–5.

13 J. Pickard (1990) 'When pay gets personal', *Personnel Management*, 22 (7): 41–5.

14 N. Nicholson and M. West (1988) *Managerial Job Change: Men and Women in Transition*. Cambridge: Cambridge University Press.

15 P. Evans and F. Bartolome (1980) *Must Success Cost so Much?* London: Grant McIntyre.

16 U. Sekaran and D.T. Hall (1989) 'Asynchronism in dual-career and family linkages', in M.B. Arthur, D.T. Hall and B.S. Lawrence (eds), *Handbook of Career Theory*. Cambridge: Cambridge University Press.

17 H. Rosin (1990) 'Consequences for men of dual career marriages: implications for organisations', *Journal of Managerial Psychology*, 5: 76–88.

9

Knowledge and Tolerance

The need for professionals

Many of the business trends of the 90s are technology driven:

- The development of new products and services involves technologies, often in combination.
- Product obsolescence requires greater collaboration within R&D and between R&D and other functions.
- The development of information technology makes it possible to integrate the product/service cycle within the organisation.
- Information technology provides feedback for the customer/client/consumer to the organisation and to its suppliers.
- Many of the core competences of organisations are based on this integrative know-how.

Technical and professional knowledge will consequently be at a premium, and its owners will be in great demand. Many organisations however, will feel that they can't afford to attract and retain such people. It is not just what they cost; it's the hassle they cause as well. After all, most people seem to think that the Mr Spocks of the organisational world:

- don't understand the needs of the business;
- go for perfection rather than marketability;
- are terribly touchy about ethics;
- get their best Brownie points outside the organisation;
- value what their peers rather than their superiors think of them;
- make themselves more marketable at others' expense;
- won't be managed by anyone other than one of their own;
- don't want to manage people or budgets;
- ignore administrative procedures;
- won't collaborate with other people;
- can't communicate with them either;
- don't wear ties and pick their nose.

So why have them? Some organisations are giving up on them. They're following the predictions of Charles Handy, who thinks that organisations will be shaped like the clover leaf: a core of generalists who have a job for life; a portfolio of professionals whom the organisation can hire for one-off assignments; and people doing manual jobs who are paid wages over the short term.[1]

This may be a current trend in the face of recession. But the survivor organisations of the year 2000 won't be the clover leaves. On the contrary, clover will have been mowed down. The top 200 of the year 2000 will have chosen and refined their core competencies. These are what gives them their cutting edge as they mow down the opposition. Many of their core competencies are their know-how about how to use technology to integrate their functions or get feedback from their customers. This know-how is vested in their experts and professionals. It takes time to acquire, and it's *very* precious to competitors. How can it possibly be entrusted to Johnny-come-lately mercenaries of the mind? Despite Kanter,[2] specialists *do* have some organisation-specific knowledge; they don't merely travel with their professional skills packed into their c.v. Yes, organisations have to attract them in – but then they have to retain them.

So, like it or not, organisations have to find a space for professionals and experts. They don't merely have to find a space – they have to furnish an intellectual play-room for them. But first, they have to understand what sort of people they are and what sort of career they want.

Professional careers

Building on their earlier work, Gene Dalton and Paul Thompson have given us the best account yet.[3] They interviewed 550 US professionals in all: 155 scientists in four R&D laboratories; 268 engineers in four organisations; 52 accountants in three accountancy practices; and 75 academics in three universities. Dalton and Thompson identified four career stages for these professionals, with the following percentages falling into each: Stage 1: 13.4; Stage 2: 46.2; Stage 3: 29.3; Stage 4: 11.1. The four stages were defined in terms of the following criteria:

Stage 1
- is supervised by a more senior professional;
- is never responsible for a project as a whole;
- does most of the detailed and routine work;
- is directed on how to demonstrate initiative.

Stage 2
- is expert in one area;
- takes responsibility for a part of a project;
- works independently of a supervisor and/or mentor;
- gets a reputation.

Stage 3
- works in more than one area;
- has a breadth of skills and their application;
- develops other professionals;
- deals with client organisations.

Stage 4
- influences the organisation's decisions;
- provides strategic insights;
- represents the organisation internally and externally;
- sponsors individuals for key positions.

In sum: Stage 1 is apprenticeship.
       Stage 2 is independence.
       Stage 3 is mentoring.
       Stage 4 is strategic.

What is really surprising is the ages of those at each stage. The ages in Stage 1 ranged from 21 to 60, and averaged 39. The average ages of Stages 2 and 3 were 41.4, and of Stage 4, 42.7. Average performance ratings were in the order $4>3>2>1$, so the organisation values the more advanced stages. And within Stages 1 and 2, younger professionals were rated higher than older ones, so an age-stage expectation was operating. People aged 60 aren't expected to be apprentices.

There were cases of professionals regressing from Stage 3 to Stage 2 or even 1; but in most cases people simply stuck at Stage 1 or Stage 2 (usually the latter), whether by choice or by failure to make a desired transition. These patterns were similar across the organisations researched, but there was one major difference. In some organisations, only those designated 'manager' reached Stages 3 and 4. In others many non-managers did so. In one particular R&D organisation, 77 per cent of Stage 3 and 30 per cent of Stage 4 professionals were non-managers.

Making the transition from one stage of a professional career to the next is clearly a problem. How do you get properly into an apprenticeship in the first place? How do you get from apprenticeship through to independent status? How is the move from self-management to mentoring others to be negotiated? And how can one exercise strategic influence and power as a professional?

Successful professionals in Dalton and Thompson's sample *got started* by:

- getting themselves a good mentor;
- landing a challenging first assignment;
- rapidly becoming competent.

They *moved into Stage 2* by:

- becoming independent of their mentor;
- developing a professional identity and involvement;
- focusing on an area of expertise.

Those who *achieved Stage 3* had:

- assumed project, team and client management tasks;
- stopped worrying about being overtaken in their speciality;
- started surrendering 'their own' time to others.

If you made it *into Stage 4*, you had:

- agreed to go into general management, (75 per cent) *or*:
- directed a programme vital to the organisation's success;
- sponsored or yourself innovated a major new product;
- provided a new and useful set of ideas which affected the organisation as a whole;
- abandoned your professional distaste for power and politics.

What sense are we to make of these data? Clearly, the notion of 'stage' doesn't imply a steady progression over one's working life. There were those at Stages 3 and 4 who were under 30! Rather, we seem to be talking about different levels of operating, each one a necessary but not a sufficient condition for the next. Moreover, these levels can't solely be seen in terms of *individual* functioning; they have to be put into an *organisational* context. Even in a research laboratory or a law firm there need to be more Indians than chiefs. The point about being a professional is that you can be a very honourable Indian. Or you can opt out of organisational employment and develop a portfolio professional career.

Professionals tend to be driven by the need for autonomy and independence. Their satisfaction comes from the work itself, and from the esteem of their peers. This means that most will want to function at least at Stage 2, since that is the level at which they can work independently; some may choose to remain at Stage 1, since it permits them to do highly specific tasks which interest them. It is clear, then, that professionals are unlikely to find the skills of self-management required at Stage 2 hard to acquire; most succeed in doing so.

Moving to Stage 3 is another matter. Stage 3 requires many more skills of a social and managerial nature. Above all it means a loss of independence, since when people are dependent on you, you can't be independent of them. It may also mean a loss of pre-eminence in a specific area of expertise. On the other hand team leaders often get (or take) much of the credit for their colleagues' contributions.

Given that professionals will only be managed by one of their own kind whom they hold in high esteem, it's likely that professional expertise will be the primary criterion for moving to Stage 3. The social and managerial skills required at this stage may not have been acquired or 'come naturally'. Indeed, the interests and motivations of scientists and engineers are investigative, whereas those of managers are enterprising and social.[4] Or, in terms of Schein's Career Anchors (pp. 59–60), they are likely to have technical/functional and autonomy/independence anchors, rather than the anchor of managerial competence. There is, therefore, a considerable danger that those at Stage 3 may not possess the necessary skills to the required level. They may also find themselves blocking the path of thrusting young colleagues, but unable to revert to Stage 2 because they're out of date.

Many professionals are irked by their inability to influence the direction of the organisation. They see decisions being taken which reflect a lack of appreciation of technical change and its implications for the business. But few of them operate at Stage 4 to exercise a strategic influence. To do so needs:

- understanding of the business in its environment;
- knowledge of the politics of power in the organisation;
- a network of contacts beyond one's professional area;
- credibility with those with power.

Of those professionals at Stage 4, 75 per cent were, strictly speaking, ex-professionals, since they had become general managers. On the other hand, the remainder used their intellectual, expert and professional power as a lever.

Perhaps the picture we get from Dalton and Thompson's research is a little too individualised. Especially at Stage 2, we get the impression of lots of prickly individuals doing their own thing. In fact, of course, in modern organisations they work in teams, and the teams they work in are often composed of a wide variety of experts. Collaboration and communication with people other than one's immediate professional peers are required of most professionals in organisational settings. Where the autonomy and independence come in is in terms of the freedom both to define and to solve problems in the way the individual *or the team* thinks best.

And there's the rub. The organisation wants applied knowledge to help it meet its business objectives. The professionals demand tolerance and freedom to get on with it in their own way. Our third balance, that between *knowledge and tolerance*, is a hard one to strike and a harder one still to keep.

Organisations that survive will do so by maintaining and applying their core competencies. They will seek to attract and retain those professionals who will limit themselves to work within the prescribed areas. The idea of defining one's problem area for oneself is a luxury in these organisations. On the other hand, the question still needs to be asked of these organisations: are your present core competencies always going to be those on which your success depends? If not, where are the new ones coming from? How are they going to be developed? Surely such strategic decisions cannot be taken without Stage 4 professional input.

Nevertheless, the balance seems to be achievable, if at all, by distinguishing strongly between the *what* and the *how*. The what will consist of a boundary line drawn around present and projected core competencies. The how will be left totally up to the professionals.

Experts may not be professionals

There is a major challenge which we must make to the key concept of this chapter thus far – the concept of *professional*. Professions are essentially exclusive. They require a lengthy formal accreditation procedure, which has two purposes. The overt one is to ensure that they are fit to practise. The covert one is to limit numbers. More and more professions are seeking to enhance their status by limiting entry to graduates. It follows that the availability of professionals is limited more and more to the output of higher education. And because employing graduates gives status, many precious professionals are seduced into other careers. Some 250 of our engineering graduates become accountants each year.

Graduates in the UK come from the same middle-class socio-economic background as their predecessors. In one sense, therefore, organisations are limiting themselves to a small pool of the talent lake if they go for *professionals*. The surviving organisations of the year 2000 won't be going only for professionals; they'll be going for *experts*. All professionals are experts; but not all experts are professionals.

Experts don't just know a great deal about something; it's how they use their knowledge that matters. Michael Prietula and Herb Simon give a clear account of the psychology of being an expert – the processes involved in making expert judgements.[5] First, how do you become an expert? The answer is that there are no short cuts. 'Expertise is based on a deep knowledge of the problems that continually arise on a particular job. It is accumulated over years of experience tackling these problems', insist Prietula and Simon.

But how, specifically, does all this experience help? It enables the experts to overcome various limitations of the human mind. We're limited by the more peripheral parts of our thinking apparatus. We can pay attention to only a few things at the same time and move them around in our working memory. It is often hard to retrieve things from our central long-term memory where we've stored all our information, ideas and experiences. If you don't use a person's name with some frequency, you find it hard to recall it even though you know it.

The expert minimises these limitations. He or she chunks bits of information into large units, then automatically runs off the bits without having to pay attention. The car driver runs off sequences of gear changes without thinking about it. The chess grand master has a repertoire of 50,000 chunks (sequences of moves). Because experts operate in chunks, they can more easily spot various regularities and patterns in the problems that come up. This enables them to categorise types of problem and generate types of solution to them.

Experts usually do all this intuitively. That is, they don't spell out their logic in spotting the patterns of problem. This could be because the process is too fast to spell out consciously; because they don't have ways of expressing what it is they are doing; or perhaps because it is not accessible to their conscious thinking at all. A few customs officers have hit rates at spotting drug smugglers which are many times better than those of their colleagues, and far beyond the variation to be expected on the basis of chance. Yet they can't explain what cues they are processing in their decisions to search. Observers cannot identify them either.

What is done intuitively by experts depends on prior analysis, insist Prietula and Simon. At some stage in their career, experts *did* have to pay slow and careful analytic attention to information. Even now they may need to analyse alternative intuitive solutions and consciously decide which is preferable. And while the results may justify the means, they still have to try to explain to their apprentices and bosses how and why they came to their intuitive decision. The incredible difficulty they find in doing so has resulted in the short cut of expert systems: ways of tapping experts' knowledge about classes of problem without spelling out completely the logic of their solutions. It may also explain their value – no one else can do what they do without serving a similar apprenticeship.

Much of this expertise is exercised at points where different processes in the organisation make contact with each other; how problems of scheduling, co-ordination, and co-operation may best be solved. Expertise is crucial to organisations which focus on their core competencies, for co-ordination of the elements of a core competence, and its transformation into core products, are of the essence. Pragmatic experts are the application cadre of core competencies.

The value of experts is immense, but they are in danger of being undervalued. Their expertise depends on their being in the same job for quite a long time. Yet this is a definition of failure in many organisations. As Prietula and Simon put it, 'this situation is heavy with irony, since it's in the corporation's interest to cultivate and retain the talent that is essential for its survival and profitability'. However, as they note, few organisations structure their compensation and reward systems to permit superior performers to become more valuable as they stay put. 'People should be given the opportunity to become masters of important tasks without feeling that their jobs are dead ends.' Fancy ever calling such experts deadwood, just because they've been in the same job in the same organisation for a long time. The people who devalue them certainly don't possess their unconscious competence, nor their conscious competence. They're not even conscious of their own incompetence.

There is another difference between professionals and experts. Experts can be found anywhere in the organisation; professionals only in certain parts and at certain levels. Here are some experts:

- The shop assistant who knows when to bend the rules about refunds as a result of her experience of a wide range of customers.
- The publisher who can spot a winner, or the editor who judges a story newsworthy.
- The sales representative who understands what is causing customers to resist a product.
- The supervisor who knows which subordinates to team together for a project.
- The secretary to whom everyone goes for advice on word-processing.
- The manager who senses that a subordinate is under a lot of stress from non-work sources.

- The systems consultant who quickly spots the bugs in a newly installed system.
- The market researcher who knows immediately the right questions to ask in a survey.

The yin and yang of innovation

These people are indispensable because they know what to do, rather than having to find out by costly trial and error or time-consuming research. But this is not their only value. Another is their potential for *innovation*. Together with professionals, experts provide the main source of innovation in organisations. The balance between the organisation's use of applied knowledge and its tolerance of know-how people is reflected in the process of innovation: how do you permit and encourage diversity but then select only what is most useful to the organisation? It is only those organisations that achieve the knowledge–tolerance balance which will innovate successfully; conversely, it's only where innovation is part of the fabric of organisational life that experts are happy.

So what do we know about innovation? It's worth distinguishing the *process* of innovating from its *products*. The products may be new physical products or services, designed for the external market; or they may be new processes, systems or structures for internal organisational use. The latter become the former: IBM developed robots for its own use, then sold them. The innovative product may be thought of and developed entirely within the organisation, or it may be to a greater or lesser extent imported from outside. But it's the process of innovation rather than specific innovative products that's important if an organisation is to foster innovation. We can all think of large organisations which have taken over small creative businesses and killed the goose that laid the golden eggs. Why? Because they did not foster the innovative process – it wasn't in their culture to do so.

In a brilliant chapter, Barry Staw has counterposed the yin and yang of the innovation process: the need to generate a large number of different innovative ideas and the countervailing need to select from among them those that best meet the organisation's objectives.[6] It will become increasingly important to get the innovation balance right in the 90s. Technology will not be enough; to gain competitive advantage, new products and services to capture market niches and new systems and structures to support them will be generated by the creativity of employees. Even the blue-chip analyser academies of the organisational world have difficulties in coping with the rate of obsolescence of products and services and the demand for new ones.

So what will be the successful yin and yang of the process of innovation in the survivors of the 90s? Kanter identifies certain protective procedures in successful innovative organisations.[7] The little seedlings of ideas are sheltered from premature exposure to a frosty reception from various organisational controls:

- Projects can be financed from slack, and so avoid formalised budgetary procedures.
- Individual members of teams can be given time to pursue personal ideas.
- Powerful protectors can ward off political pressure from threatened parties.
- Budgets and accountability for their use can be decentralised and controlled by a sponsor.

This is not to say that the seedlings need to be hothouse plants for the rest of their lives. In order to survive in the harsh world of competition, ideas have to:

- obtain resources from stakeholders;
- be evaluated according to agreed organisational criteria;
- accept a more formal accountability.

But the early protection is necessary to give a balance, since seedlings tend to be stamped upon before they've had a chance to show their potential. Among organisational processes of control, those which are especially likely to stamp out creative ideas prematurely are:

- narrowly defined job descriptions;
- short-term bottom-line accounting;
- frequent evaluation of performance according to the achievement of routine objectives;
- controlling rather than supportive management processes.

Innovative ideas

But all this is at the early development, rather than the initial germination stage. Where do the seeds come from? How are numerous and varied ideas brought to birth? We're handicapped in our thinking about thinking by the romantic myth – the notion of the mad genius, the Van Gogh of the laboratory. Innovative ideas usually have a *social* origin; they don't spring fully-formed from the head of the genius. Among these social influences are:

- a problem as the source of an idea: people from inside the organisation or customers may have voiced a difficulty or a need;
- colleagues who encourage freewheeling speculation and spark each other off;
- competitors who are already doing something innovative;
- dissenters in a group who form a minority: such dissenters stimulate more solutions, of a wider variety.

Here again, the yin and the yang are in evidence. The ideas come from people with such a knowledge and experience of their area that they've already been internally censored. Experts often know in principle what's needed without spelling out how they've arrived at their conclusion. And they're likely to have limited the scope of their solutions to what they know is feasible. So the selectivity, the yin, has already been applied in the expert's or the group's minds. It has inhibited the yang of the generation of ideas. Sometimes this is quite appropriate; really novel solutions aren't necessary. But sometimes the individual's and the group's mental constraints need to be put in abeyance for a while. This is where brainstorming and lateral thinking techniques come in useful; they encourage idea generation and expression, postponing evaluation till later. People can feel safe to produce a wide variety of ideas; and they can be sure that the collective expertise and vision will subsequently winnow them out to leave only quality innovation.[8]

Minority dissent in a group also helps generate idea variety,[9] but subsequently a unified group is more likely to push through implementation successfully.[10] Again the yin and yang of innovation are evident – idea generation followed by selection of and concentration on a preferred alternative.

Supporting innovation

Different roles need to be played here. The organisation will benefit from:

- *idea champions*, who are prepared to put extraordinary effort into gaining support for an idea (not necessarily their own);[11]
- *expert critics*, who can see why an idea won't work, or who can foresee unintended consequences because they know the system;[12]
- *idea generators*, for whom having new ideas rather than putting them into practice is all-important;
- *inventors*, for whom the opposite is true; their challenge is to put ideas into tangible form.

Again, these roles involve both generating ideas in varied profusion *and* evaluating them. The role of critic is too often downplayed, and is itself criticised as 'resistance'.[13] Resistance is often justified – people know, because they are experts, that something won't work, at least as it stands. They are often in subordinate positions, and they are often disregarded. They're not necessarily hostile to new ideas in general – they are hostile to this one in particular, and for very good reasons. Their role is indeed crucial: it's got to be played at the right time, though. Not too soon, to stifle variety; not too late, when a lot of harm's been done already.

We're not just talking about technical experts here; there are also organisational experts, (who may also be Scotties). They will be able to understand the organisational consequences of innovation. It is organisational innovations which are more likely to fail, since they will have numerous system constraints and unexpected outcomes. A growing industry in open conferences rests on the fact that people are eager to pick up organisational innovations from those who have tried them. Quality circles are an example. To implant quality circles into an organisation without any history of consultative procedures or values is to invite failure. To ignore the need for a mechanism to ensure that proposals are acted upon is to disregard organisational context. Yet still organisations embrace isolated innovations inappropriate for them now.

This brings us to the nub of the innovation debate. Few innovations can stand on their own. For example, technical innovations usually founder unless they are supported by corresponding organisational changes. Information technology was introduced into offices in the 1970s and 1980s often without the redesign of jobs and without the systems necessary to support it. The survivor organisations of the year 2000 will not be those which make good but isolated individual innovations. They will be innovative organisations. The innovations won't come from a few boffins in R&D and corporate strategy; they will come from any individual or group with expertise. It may not be the technical innovations which are in the end so crucial to survival as the organisational ones. We may not have a viable European electronics industry in the year 2000, for example, unless the few electronics giants collaborate in forging the same formidable partnerships with government and banks as their Japanese competitors already possess.

Here's an example of organisational and technical innovations combined. A financial services organisation had a need for training its staff, many of whom were women returners in isolated branch offices. It had a high staff turnover of around 20 per cent p.a. Its decision in the late 1970s was to use computer-based training, running on the large computer that was used to support the business through terminals in all branches. The organisation acquired the rights to a computer-based training (CBT) authoring system and started writing materials. The next step was to offer this service to other organisations on a bureau basis and then to support it with consultancy. Eventually it set up a subsidiary company to market CBT, identified and acquired a more up-to-date authoring system running on a personal computer, and improved it to the point where it was competitive in the market-place. The CBT business became a major player with a large production capability, noted for its efficiency (and for rather boring learning materials).

However, as the business grew in turnover (but not in profit-ability) it became more bureaucratic. Its smaller competitors were more agile and it was unable to find a third-generation product. The company was sold, integrated with a rival and is now a second-rate player. It is unlikely to survive to 2000.

What systems favouring innovation will we see in the survivor organisations?

- rewards of greater autonomy and more resources to innovative teams and experts (since they tend to have autonomy and technical/functional career anchors);
- recruitment which stresses the learning opportunities of working with world leaders in their field;
- public recognition of the contribution made by innovators at whatever level in the organisation;
- a mechanism for involving experts in decision-making at the organisational level;
- clear criteria for deciding which innovations to implement;
- appropriate training for moving into the next stage of a professional career: for example time management and team leadership training for Stage 2 (independence) and Stage 3 (mentoring) respectively;
- career discussions, which don't assume a managerial career anchor and therefore promotion to general management as an aim.[14]

Some final questions

About your own career

- Are you a professional? Which of others' perceptions of professionals listed on p. 136 are current in your own organisation? Which of them are accurate perceptions of you and your colleagues?

- At which of Dalton and Thompson's four stages of professional development are you at present? Are you happy there, or do you want to move? What's stopping you, and why?
- Are you an expert? What is your expertise? How long did it take to acquire? What would happen to the organisation if it wasn't exercised?
- Think of an occasion when you had an innovative idea. What happened to it, and why?

About your organisation

- In what ways, if any, does your organisation help its professionals to move from one career stage to another?
- To what extent does your organisation understand and value its experts? How does it give them recognition?
- How good is your organisation at innovating? How does it nurture innovative ideas (if at all)?
- Think of one technical and one organisational innovation that have taken place in your organisation recently. Where did they come from? Who introduced them? Who got them accepted, and how?

Notes

1 C. Handy (1989) *The Age of Unreason*. London: Business Books.

2 R.M. Kanter (1989) 'The new managerial work', *Harvard Business Review*, 89 (6): 85–92.

3 G.W. Dalton, P.H. Thompson and R. Price (1977) 'The four stages of professional careers', *Organisational Dynamics*, Summer: 19–42; G. Dalton and P. Thompson (1989) *Novations: Strategies for Career Management*. Glenview, Illinois: Scott, Foresman.

4 J.L. Holland (1973) *Making Vocational Choices: A Theory of Careers*. Englewood Cliffs, NJ: Prentice-Hall.

5 M.J. Prietula and H.A. Simon (1989) 'The expert in your midst', *Harvard Business Review*, 89 (1): 120–4.

6 B. Staw (1990) 'An evolutionary approach to creativity and innovation', in M.A. West and J.L. Farr (eds) *Innovation and Creativity at Work*. Chichester, Sussex: Wiley.

7 R.M. Kanter (1983) *The Change Masters*. New York: Simon & Schuster.

8 J.L. Farr (1990) 'Facilitating individual role innovation', in M.A. West and J.L. Farr (eds), *Innovation and Creativity at Work*. Chichester, Sussex: Wiley.

9 C. Nemeth (1986) 'Differential contributions of majority and minority influence', *Psychological Review*, 93: 23–32.

10 H. Nystrom (1979) *Creativity and Innovation*. New York: Wiley.

11 R. Bouwen and R. Fry (1988) 'An agenda for managing organisation

innovation and development in the 1990s', in M. Lambrecht (ed.), *Corporate Revival*. Leuven: Catholic University Press.

12 G. Zaltman and R. Duncan (1977) *Strategies for Planned Change*. New York: Wiley.

13 E.M. Rogers (1983) *Diffusion of Innovations*, 3rd edn. New York: Free Press.

14 C.B. Derr (1986) *Managing the New Careerists*. San Francisco: Jossey-Bass.

10

Intelligence and Trust

The dual function of the core people

Last but not least, Lieutenant Uhura. But that's what they all say. The order in which people are mentioned is revealing. In yesterday's newspaper, a hospital which ridiculously believes that efficiency and effectiveness are the same thing reported the categories of staff which it was making redundant: managers (a few), administrators, technical staff and nurses (a lot). In that order. Last on this list came the people who are at the core of the organisation. They provide the health care which is its *raison d'être*. Nurses, salespersons, teachers, maintenance engineers . . . all are core people who are expected to provide intelligence in carrying out the basic mission of the organisation.

What's crucial about these employees is that their intelligence is exercised directly upon the customer or client. It is used in face-to-face situations. Further intelligence is gained from these same encounters. Meeting the client and providing the service is their arena *both* for using their own knowledge *and* for acquiring more for the organisation.

- The *nurse* understands that this patient needs to have the details of the treatment and its rationale spelt out in considerable detail. She uses her understanding of patients' needs and her technical knowledge of the treatment to explain them to him. She also realises that requests for such detailed explanation have become more frequent recently. Since the treatment is a common one and a large number of patients undergo it in her ward, she tells the senior registrar and suggests that a detailed preparatory briefing for groups of patients could be instituted.
- *Desk staff* at the travel agent listen patiently to a customer's vague fantasies about holidays in the sun. They know exactly which questions to ask, and in what order, to discover whether there's anything available within shouting distance of what she appears to want. People keep coming along these days with a new mixture of demands. They seem to want all the hassle taken out of getting there and getting back; they want a car

laid on and domestic comforts when they arrive. But they want danger and excitement once they're there. The desk staff report this trend to the holiday company's marketeers, who make a point of visiting the travel agent regularly to discover what customers want but can't get.

- The *teacher* is discussing careers with several of his students. He realises that they all share the same misapprehension about the training and qualifications needed for a job as a car mechanic. Understanding their leisure habits, he unearths in discussion a source of the false impression – a currently popular soap opera made abroad. He phones the local technical college to tell them of the misunderstanding about the training requirements for this occupation, and suggests a new format for their course brochure which explicitly corrects the error.

- The *computer engineer* is called out frequently to mend a newly marketed model. She rapidly discovers the fault, and notes that this same fault occurs often. On questioning the users, she discovers that they have all been tampering with the machine to try to make a certain function possible which was not available on the machine as sold. She decides to mend the computers in such a way as to continue to permit the function, although this is contrary to the manual. She reports these incidents back to Design and to Marketing. To Design, because it will take a relatively minor adjustment in production to provide the required function. To Marketing because it seems strange at first sight to want the two functions together – perhaps there are new uses to which computers of this size are being put: a potential niche market beckons.

So Lieutenant Uhura isn't just a very skilled navigator who is trusted with the starship's course – she also interprets the signals from surrounding space and reports them back to Kirk.

All of the employees in our examples felt free to do things which were appropriate in the situation but probably weren't strictly by the book. The maths teacher gave careers advice; the nurse gave the level of medical explanation usually reserved to doctors; and the computer engineer mended the computers according to the customers' needs rather than the manual's instructions. Each of them exercised autonomy in their decisions – they acted as they did because it helped their customer or client. Recall the British Airways cabin staff (pp. 88–90). They could only start really serving the customers when most of the rules about how they ought to serve the customers were abolished.

As we saw in chapter 2, information technology can deal with all the programmable aspects of service. What isn't programmable is the unique response to each individual customer's perceived needs. This is why in a few years' time robots will quite happily recognise customers' spoken requests and 'say' the appropriate thing as recommended by some of the worst customer-care training packages. But it will still take people to develop the individual local solutions. Flexibility is the name of the game, which is why decision-making and budgetary responsibility have been devolved way down the line in many organisations.

But our heroes each spotted the significance of what they saw; so they reported it back to others who could put it into the context of the whole organisation. The people who deal with the client or customer are gatekeepers. They are at the same time the *core*, the central players in the achievement of the mission, and the *boundary*, since they interface with the outside world. So their role is doubly important – they do the work by which the organisation survives or fails now, and they provide the sort of information on which its survival depends in the future.

Many organisations are coming to recognise this. Popular management texts tell of organisations hyping up these heroes of the front line.[1] The survivors of the year 2000 won't just be calling them heroes. They will have changed their culture, their structure and their systems so that everyone else supports them.

Obstacles in the way

What happens now? Here are a few imbalances between structure and culture:

Decentralised structures but lack of trust
Managerial and budgetary responsibilities are nominally passed down the line. However, the accountability is emphasised and control is exercised from above. Budgetary control from the centre is tight and restrictive. Frequent reports have to be made back with the figures, with detailed budget heads and no latitude for transfer. Managers of fast-food outlets, for example, tend to have accountability but little real discretion. Relinquishing day-to-day control in order to ensure local flexibility is a hard lesson for senior management to learn.

Reporting in but no disclosure
Messages from the coal face are expected and asked for. But there's no communication outward of marketing strategy. Our

travel agency clerk and computer engineer interpreted their experience with their customers strategically. They saw its significance in terms of gaps in existing market strategy. They could only do so because they understood existing market strategy. But these were idealised examples. The prevalent situation is, as Alastair Mant sadly reports, that 'the people who invent the markets hardly ever meet the people who serve them'.[2] The marketeers who promise quality, consistency and brand image, and the deliverers of those promises, have but a nodding acquaintance with each other.

Information down, but no reporting in
The internal communications industry has grown fat in recent years. Management discloses changes and results already achieved, and sometimes reveals some strategic intentions too. It also commissions attitude surveys to discover levels of employee satisfaction with, among other things, internal communications. Worthwhile though these efforts are, organisations may be lacking the most important information of all – what the client wants now or might want in the future.

Consultative machinery, but no real consultation
Mick Marchington notes that there are all sorts of reasons for holding joint consultative committees.[3] One may be to prevent unionisation by persuading employees that management is managing effectively and is committed to the overall benefit of the company and its employees. Another reason may be to decrease remaining union power by bypassing union representatives and going direct to the employees; yet another to present the appearance of consultation but permit the discussions to degenerate to trivia. Finally, joint consultative committees can act as an adjunct to collective bargaining. They can be concerned with real problems of a strategic nature, but will probably be seen as advisory rather than decision-making. None of these models, except perhaps the last, is concerned to use employees' knowledge and ideas in taking strategic decisions.

Customer-first programmes but boss-first practice
It's possible to persuade people who deal directly with customers who their customers are, and it's not hard to show them additional ways of discovering customers' needs and meeting them. It's a lot harder to do the same for those who don't deal directly with the customer. Currently, customer-care, client-first or total-quality programmes tell these people that their client is anyone in the organisation as well as those outside it.[4] This is a sure-fire recipe

for preserving the status quo, since bosses will continue to get priority. Internal priority will be given by the year 2000 survivors to those who provide the service, not to the boss.

The gap between where most organisations are and where they will have to be is immense. In terms of real delegation of power and responsibility to the coal face, current strategic constraints pull hard in the opposite direction. Many organisations are seeking to move from defender to analyser mode. They have decentralised structurally, but are struggling to kick the habit of detailed corporate control. However, the current recession has forced many down into reactor mode (see Figure 6.1, p. 83), where centralised decision-making aimed solely at survival is the order of the day. Immediate survival requires centralisation, long-term survival *de*centralisation within the core competencies framework.

In this recessionary context, the European Community agenda of employees' rights to information, to participation in board decisions, and to a financial stake in the organisation appears at first sight irrelevant.[5] Yet it may be the last opportunity for many organisations to consider longer- as well as shorter-term issues of survival. As Rex Adams notes,[6] where these formal steps towards participation have been taken in the UK, 'employee directors have spread their knowledge of how the businesses work, and the external influences upon them, in a very useful way in times of commercial and economic difficulty'. Or, to quote Nigel Nicholson and colleagues' report of their research findings on the UK textile industry,

> In every one of our case companies, there had been at least one employee who had revealed an acute understanding of the most pressing problems facing the company and been able to suggest plausible and inventive solutions to them. These individuals, however, were usually in low visibility organisational positions, at the sharp receiving end of company problems, from whence voices were seldom heard at the top. This is an insight that all companies would do well to bear in mind. No matter how passive or restricted may appear the roles of employees in relation to organisational objectives, most nevertheless do have active conceptions of their environment and how it could be improved. Underlying this is a store of local wisdom and inventiveness. If organisations can unblock the traditional inhibitions of free-flowing ideas and opinions the constructive change may be closer to hand than might appear.[7]

There exists a variety of reasons apart from the recession why participation is so patchy in the UK. Among them are:

- a belief that the professional expertise of managers is that of decision-making;

- a belief than non-management employees can't take a longer-term view;
- a fear of loss of power, authority, status and effectiveness;
- a suspicion that the value priorities of non-managerial employees will be different, for example about the relative importance of profit, authority and equity.

But employers in Europe and Japan accept a body of workers' rights, including tenured wage scales, employment guarantees and investment in training, as well as participation in decision-making. As Will Hutton observes,[8] one of the benefits that these employers enjoy as a consequence is the co-ordination of wage-bargaining across the economy. But such a large-scale exchange of benefits requires industry associations such as the CBI to play a proactive role in discussing these possibilities with the TUC. It also requires unions to collaborate with each other within and across sectors in ways they have failed to achieve in the past.

Such *institutional* arrangements seem to sit uncomfortably with the major thrust of this book: that *individuals* differ in what they expect from their organisational careers, and that organisations will need to take account of these differences if they are to achieve their business objectives. But unions too depend much more nowadays for their survival upon serving the varied needs of their members. Those needs extend far wider than wage bargaining. Where they do relate to rewards, it is the monetary *value* of the reward package, together with the freedom to 'spend' that value how they wish, for which unions will bargain on behalf of their members.

So what sort of *systems* will support the intelligence–trust balance?

- delegated authority to local managers to manage their own budgets without central interference; and overall targets set in consultation at regular but widely spaced intervals;
- delegated authority to sharp-end employees to use their intelligence to serve the customer or client to the highest standards;
- active searching out of successful local initiatives for customers and their dissemination throughout the organisation;
- systems for recognising and rewarding these initiatives;
- widespread discussion and dissemination of organisational strategy, especially of marketing strategy;
- detailed local discussion on how local units fit into the strategy, and how it needs to be adapted to their particular situation;
- active acquisition of local information about customers which is pertinent to strategy;

- collection and dissemination of such customer information, and its use in developing marketing strategy;
- joint consultative committees which can bring together sharp-end market knowledge and knowledge of the corporate business environment;
- appraisal criteria which reward managers for the extent to which they support their subordinates.

Some final questions

About your own career

- How regularly do you come into contact with your organisation's external customers or clients?
- To what extent do you find yourself constrained by company policies or norms in your attempts to meet their needs? List the constraints – why are they there? Do they need to be there? How might they be relaxed?
- Think of a couple of recent meetings with customers. What did you learn from them about the customer? What *could* you have learned about? Why didn't you?
- Are you ever asked for customer information by someone in your organisation? Do you ever volunteer it? Are there any possible systems for facilitating information flow?

About your organisation

- What are your organisation's basic products or services? Who provides them, and to whom?
- What is the degree of local variation in your market? What degree of discretion do local employees have to adapt to that variation – in operational terms? In budgeting terms?
- How aware are local employees of the organisation's strategy, especially its marketing strategy, as it applies to their unit?
- What systematic efforts are made to collect and use local customer information? How often do local employees transfer to other localities or to central roles?

Notes

1 R.M. Kanter (1989) *When Giants Learn to Dance.* New York: Simon & Schuster; T.J. Peters and R.H. Waterman (1981) *In Search of Excellence.* New York: Harper & Row.

2 A. Mant (1990) 'Customer service: What do clients really want?' *Personnel Management*, 22 (10): 38–43.

3 M. Marchington (1988) 'The four faces of employee consultation', *Personnel Management*, 20 (5): 44–7.

4 E. Giles and R. Williams (1991) 'Can the personnel department survive quality management?', *Personnel Management*, 23 (4): 28–33.

5 C. Mill (1991) 'The long road to employee involvement', *Personnel Management*, 23 (2): 26–7.

6 R. Adams (1984) *Participation Today*. Gateshead: The Industrial Participation Association and Northumberland Press. (Quote from p. 154).

7 N. Nicholson, A. Rees and A. Brooks-Rooney (1990) 'Strategy, innovation and performance', *Journal of Management Studies*, 27 (5): 511–34. (Quote from p. 531).

8 W. Hutton (1991) *The Guardian*, 29 April.

11
Individuals and Organisations

This has been a book about business; about how businesses will survive over the next decade in the face of competition, internationalisation, technological change and mergers and recession. It is therefore a hard-nosed book, since it addresses the most urgent medium- and long-term issue which faces them: how to be around in the year 2000.

Yet it appears a soft and woolly book, with much more about people than about money and mechanics. Indeed, there are very few numbers at all. This is not because finance is unimportant, but because people are more important. All of the pressing business imperatives require greater expectations and demands upon employees. And these expectations will be met only if equal attention is paid to the expectations which these employees hold of the organisation.

I have not argued that a human resources strategy should be developed to support strategic business plans. Rather, that business activity by definition requires the active participation and collaboration of all employees. Since this will be achieved by agreement rather than by top-down control, it is the establishment and maintenance of such agreements which come first. This is why the central idea has been that of a career as a series of psychological contracts. Organisational missions and strategies follow from these agreements, since employees are the originators as well as the followers of organisational directions. Major changes of direction often start at the periphery rather than at the corporate centre; senior management has sensed them and given them meaning rather than initiated them.

The establishment and maintenance of agreements are tricky tasks. Balancing on a high wire isn't a bad analogy. It's a matter of continuous need to compensate should one part of the corporation lean too far to one side or the other. The continuous push for change shouldn't overweigh Kirk's need for support; Scotty's willingness to take on any job can't be taken for granted; Spock must temper his freedom to experiment with an understanding that his knowledge has to be useful; and Uhura has to merit the trust that is placed in her by keeping the organisational mission firmly in her mind.

But there also has to be an *overall* balance; it's no good keeping the head dead straight between the shoulders if the arms are all over the place. More attention in general has been paid to Kirk than to Spock; more to Spock than Uhura; and Scotty currently comes last of all. It's clear that some compensatory movements will occur as surviving organisations readjust. Probably the most urgent of these readjustments is Uhura's. For in the short and medium term the quality of her performance in meeting customers' needs flexibly is crucial to survival. For the medium term, the proper attention to and use of the information she can provide will give competitive edge in the development of new goods and services. But Scotty's balance, too will become of greater importance. As organisational change becomes ever faster, the maintaining of some sort of continuity and the interspersing of some periods of relative stability will be vital; only Scotties can do this.

The arena for choice: strategic types

But here we're already falling into the trap of concentrating on organisations and their needs. Many of the previous chapters have suffered from the same bias. To try to correct it, this chapter will be devoted to individuals. How are individuals to maintain *their* desired balance? After all, as Godfrey Golzen and Andrew Garner in their topical and perceptive book '*Smart Moves*' suggest, 'ownership of careers is being transferred from the organisation to the individual. In a career sense, we are all self-employed now.'[1] They go on to argue that this is 'the most profound change in relationships between masters and men since feudalism'. While the organisation desperately treads the tightrope to survival, adjusting its balance as it goes, many individuals can choose which most suits their preference. How may they best do so?

- The first step is to understand organisations and the state of each of the four balances within them.
- The second is to understand your own preference for one or more balances rather than others.
- The third is to try to match the two; by negotiating a new role, by finding a new organisation, or by deciding that an organisational career isn't what you want.

So your first task is to try to analyse organisations in terms of the balances they are likely to offer, a task which I started in chapter 6. My argument has been throughout that organisations will need to achieve all four balances if they are to succeed in meeting the challenges of their environment and the expectations of their employees. But this is a prescriptive posture. Which balances are actually being achieved in practice, and by what sort of organisation?

I argued in chapter 6 that organisations of certain strategic types will have appropriate HR characteristics. Defenders will have internal labour markets, as will analysers. Prospectors and reactors will, on the contrary, draw in recruits from the external market. Analysers and prospectors will concentrate on individuals' performance, clubs and reactors on groups'. Analysers, I suggested, would concentrate on developing home-grown people; prospectors on recruiting stars; defenders on retaining employees; and reactors on retrenchment. These emphases make it likely that different strategic types will have mastered some balancing tricks better than others. Let's start with defenders.

Defenders

'Clubs'. They place high values on loyalty, equity and reliability. They grow their people from within, and give them a steady progression through a career structure. They value generalised and organisation-specific experience. Obviously, the balance they have concentrated most on is that of *loyalty–rights*. Scotty is safe in their hands. It's worth noting that it is often in public-sector defender organisations that the rights of minorities are most strongly asserted.

However, unless defenders have a monopoly, they will be finding it harder and harder to hang on to their share of their specific market. Cost-efficiency may have reached its limit without damaging the product or service. Many defenders are now seeking to address their *intelligence–trust* balance. Only by offering customer-specific and superlative service will they retain their share of the market basket into which all their eggs are put. And only by paying attention to what they can learn about the customer will they keep their products and services competitive. Service organisations such as the Post Office and British Rail are seeking to address the intelligence–trust balance. But many defenders are so concerned with their functioning, with the loyalty–rights balance, that refocusing outwards is hard. Bureaucratic rules often prevent flexible customer service. So defenders tend to offer a loyalty–rights balance and, with difficulty, intelligence–trust too.

Analysers

What balances are analysers likely to offer? Analysers grow their own people by and large, and prepare them as individuals for their changing roles. This is especially true of their stars, for whom the change–support balance is well achieved. It's worth asking, though, whether the balance is equally well achieved for their solid citizens.

Similarly, with their emphasis on investigating new markets and on their core competencies, analysers often achieve a good knowledge–tolerance balance. Professional knowledge and expertise is valued and recognised. But opportunities for innovation may be limited, squashed flat by the need to evaluate every new proposal carefully.

On the other hand, sharp-end people in analyser organisations often feel powerless. The bureaucracy prevents them from exercising their judgement to meet the customer's needs. The information they can give about the real world is ignored by the high-powered central planning and strategy boffins. Hence the intelligence–trust balance is unlikely to be met.

So the balances we are most likely to find in analysers are change–support and knowledge–tolerance.

Prospectors

In prospectors, we'll probably find a mixture. Some of them, such as the small entrepreneurial companies, will guarantee knowledge-tolerance. They depend on their stars to use their expertise to invent new products or services and to discover or create new markets. The big conglomerates, on the other hand, are hot on intelligence–trust. They depend on their people in diverse businesses to run their own show, make a profit, and tell them about what's going on in their market-place. So in prospectors we may well find either the knowledge–tolerance or the intelligence-trust balance.

Reactors

Reactors are losing their balance all the time. A push from one side may hit them on the head, shoulder, trunk or legs. Invariably, the push will disturb their balance in the direction of the *firm's* demands. It wants more change, more commitment, a sudden mastery of new knowledge, or the willingness to do absolutely anything for the customer; usually all four things at the same time! The need to cut costs and simultaneously to increase productivity means that it's next to impossible to redress these imbalances. Training and development go out of the window; loyal employees are sacked; there's no tolerance of new ideas unless they're geared to survival; and the new cadre of hatchet men trust no one but themselves to do the dirty work. The only hope for reactor fortresses is to hang on by their fingernails and claw their way back to the end of the high wire. Then they can start again. Having a vision and a hope of this end in sight is vital; so many just can't see things ever improving; a black hole of despair. No balances at all here, I'm afraid.

The arena for choice: strategic shifters

But our analysis of the current scene in chapter 5 suggested that for all those organisations which could be confidently placed in one of the four strategic types, there were others which couldn't. These were the *shifters*, organisations on the move from one type to another. As a general rule, shifts disturb balances. Balances which were present in the previous state are lost sight of, while new balances aren't yet achieved. This is usually because when they change strategic type, the first thing organisations do is make new and different demands of their employees. Later they may adjust the balances towards meeting individuals' needs.

The great shifts of our time are shifts away from defender – to analyser, prospector, or reactor (see Figure 6.1, p. 83). So the loyalty–rights balance typical of defenders is often lost; as noted in chapter 1, the cradle to grave career is a thing of the past. But more generally, the long-term understanding about the rewards for long-term service are out of the window. If I am right, each of the shifts towards the new strategic types will involve a typical new demand from the organisation.

- the move to analyser will be dominated by expectations for change and for knowledge;
- the move to prospector by a requirement for environmental intelligence;
- the move to reactor by expectations of everything – all hands to the pump.

We can see all this happening already:

- would-be analysers making international forays without doing the spadework abroad or setting up the support systems at home;
- would-be prospectors making a variety of acquisitions but failing to delegate authority to these new businesses;
- enforced reactors expecting Herculean efforts from people who feel betrayed, having just lost the one balance which gave them security.

Now of course, these shifters may redress the key balances. Would-be analysers may in time build up their support systems; would-be prospectors may get round to trusting the people at the periphery and give them real autonomy; enforced reactors may drag themselves out of the mire in the long term. But the buyer should beware. Organisations aspiring to analyser or prospector status won't be offering the balances that their mature models can offer. The superb development programme of an IBM or a Shell, or the opportunity to turn around an ailing acquisition while still in your early thirties offered by Hanson, Grand Metropolitan or BAT won't be available. Aspiration and actuality are miles apart, especially when the aspiration has been hurriedly enforced by some environmental catastrophe.

So individuals need to analyse their present and potential employers. They will be looking for certain balances in particular, so they could do worse than follow the following sequence:

- Can the organisation be clearly allocated to one of the four strategic types?
- If yes, which one? Which balances does this type usually provide? Does this organisation provide them?
- If no, is the organisation making a major shift? Which one – from which type to which other type?
- Which balance is likely to have been lost in this shift?
- Which organisational demands are likely to ensue?

How are these questions to be answered? Only by acquiring a knowledge of the organisation's market and human resource strategies:

- What market(s) is the organisation aiming for?
- How does it intend to acquire/retain market share?
- Does it operate primarily with an internal or an external labour market?
- Does it concentrate on individuals or groups?
- What level of support does it offer for what degree of change?
- What level of respect does it pay for what length of loyalty?
- What level of tolerance does it allow for what amount of knowledge?
- What degree of trust does it give for what level of local intelligence?

So employees will be looking at the demands and expectations of the job, and at what they are likely to get in return. What are the training and development systems? What are the supports for transitions? How far will the organisation meet my own individual expectations? What happens to attempted innovations? How much autonomy and delegated authority will I have?

Individuals' preferred balances

But individuals will be asking other questions as well. They will be asking which balances are particularly important to *them*. For it is these balances in particular which they will be seeking to negotiate with their present or potential employer. Depending on their career anchor, their age and length of service in the organisation, their personal circumstances and a host of other variables, people are likely to prefer one sort of overall balance to another.

- Some will want to work in organisations where the change–support and knowledge–tolerance axes are emphasised.
- Others will want to give loyalty but receive reciprocal rights.
- Others again will primarily welcome the opportunity to use their intelligence in the market-place provided they are trusted to do so.

Throughout this book I've avoided trying to fit people into a single set of categories. Basically, my analysis of people has been in terms of their view of themselves or *self-concept*, and of the *roles* they are playing at any one point in their lives. Their self-concept will incorporate such things as their career anchors, their views of their own capabilities, their occupational and gender identities, and their value priorities. The roles they play may include those of citizen, spouse or partner, parent, child. Like organisations, people in my book are on the move.

While the self-concept doesn't change very fast, our current selection of roles may well be only temporary. Nevertheless, I've emphasised that people differ, and that they change. So their preferred balances at any point in time will affect the sort of contract they seek to make with their present or a new organisation.

- A post-doctoral scientist aged 26 enters her first job outside the university. She finds herself in charge of a small research team and with a project to manage. She has complete responsibility for planning, execution, meeting schedules, and budgetary control. Completely confident of her technical ability to do the work, she is searching for the change–support balance to be met, so that she can lead her team and carry the project through.
- During the course of taking five years out of work to look after a young family full-time, a woman gets divorced. She needs to work part time, and to catch up on the developments in word-processing which have occurred during her absence from work. She is certainly willing to guarantee staying with

the organisation for a reasonable period, and she is particularly keen on adequate loyalty–rights and change–support balances.

- A management accountant aged 35 has been with his organisation for ten years. He has risen through his finance department, and mastered a new and complex financial information system. He's a technical expert, and proud of it. He is now being asked to establish the use of the system in various subsidiary companies, and to train local users. He realises that the system should be modified to cater to a variety of specific needs in each of the subsidiaries. Enlisting the aid of one of the computer programmers from the IT section, he sets about adapting the system. He contemplates teaching its use to a key contact person in each of the subsidiaries. He's left his tight little professional niche: he's communicated his knowledge to others; he wants organisational recognition for his know-how – the knowledge–tolerance balance.

- The manager of a large retail store with a turnover of £20 million per year starts receiving new operating instructions from head office. The chain of which his store is a member has recently been taken over by a slightly larger chain. This has always operated very specific financial and operational control procedures, whereas his own corporate HQ simply set overall targets. He finds that many of the adaptations he has made hitherto to meet his local market's demands will be impossible within the new constraints. His intelligence–trust balance has been upset – has he any long-term prospects of readjustment? Has he any labour-market power to find another employer where the balance is achievable, or is he by now unemployable elsewhere? He's a well-respected member of the local community – he'll lose this if he moves.

A new job or a new employer?

So people and their situations change; their priorities alter. Organisations are likewise changing, many of them by huge shifts from one strategic type to another. What are employees to do in such a fluid situation? They've conducted their analysis of the organisation recommended in the first part of this chapter; they've looked at themselves, their own career anchors and life roles. Before seeking any career negotiation they need to do something else as well: they need to assess the current and likely short-term labour-market situation. Never go into a contractual negotiation without doing an analysis of strengths and weaknesses! Are they in a buyer's or a seller's labour market,[2] and how long is this market situation going to last?

These aren't easy questions to answer. They can be addressed at various levels. What's the labour market like in my particular *occupational* or functional area (both in the UK and the EC)? Electrical and mechanical engineers are scarce in the UK at present; but post-1992, will the large number of German engineers who work in the UK make it a buyer's market?

What's the labour market like in my *sector*? Management accountants may be much in demand in the flourishing food and pharmaceutical retail areas, but not in manufacturing. Whether a sector is flourishing or not can be a bigger determinant of the labour market than occupational employability.

And what's the internal labour market in my own *organisation*? If I'm a generalised middle manager, has the bloodletting of the last five years resulted in a present shortage of people like me who know how the organisation operates? Are there major strategic changes in progress which will alter the relative proportions of the workforce in each function – more marketers, less finance people, for example, or more coal-face, less corporate personnel? And where are the shortfalls or surpluses of employees at present?

So I understand the organisation, myself, and the labour market – no mean feat. What next? It's worth thinking about the possible outcomes of a career negotiation:

- no change;
- changes in my present job;
- a change of job within the organisation;
- a change of organisation;
- ceasing to work in an organisation.

I may enter the career negotiation with one of these outcomes in mind, but have to revise my expectations as I learn what the organisation expects or has to offer. 'Emergent strategy' isn't a phrase applicable only to organisations!

Job change: the realities

We have to go back once again to Nicholson and West's research to get a practical grip on what this really means for individuals.[3] When they were asked for their reasons for making their most recent job move, Nicholson and West's sample of UK managers gave the following, in decreasing order of frequency:

- to do something more challenging and fulfilling;
- I saw it as a step towards career objectives;

- to change career direction;
- to improve my standard of living;
- to acquire new skills;
- I saw no future for me in my job.

When asked for reasons, of course, people tend to attribute their job change to their own career planning. Nevertheless, we can see from this list and its order how employees renegotiate the contract (move jobs inside the organisation) or exit from it (leave the organisation). They are either seeking to better achieve a particular balance they want, or they are looking for a new balance to strike.

The boot was deliberately put onto the other foot by Nicholson and West in their next series of questions. They asked what events were associated with these job changes. The most frequent was 'business reorganisation or major organisational change'. Next comes 'a deterioration of relations at work', followed by 'involuntary loss of job'. So it looks as though upheavals in the organisation often precipitate job moves. During the course of one year in the second half of the 1980s, these managers declined overall in: the need to grow; dominance; ambition; fulfilment; confidence.

However, some of these declines occurred only for those who didn't change job during the course of the year. These stayers tended especially to become less psychologically adjusted, and to perceive less opportunities for growth. The changers, on the other hand, saw *more* growth opportunities. The overall picture is one of people getting less and less satisfied with the job that they're in, but ever hopeful that things will change in their new one. One of the things that those who moved said they had gained was greater predictability at work. That, together with the perceived greater growth opportunity, was the major consequence of the move.

When we tie this in with the circumstances surrounding their moves (reorganisation, bad relations, and actual job loss), most of the moves look to be aimed at avoiding intolerable change and uncertainty rather than at fitting in with some long-term plan. Like so much organisational 'strategy', individual career strategy seems opportunistic. On the other hand, whether or not they can make a job move within their organisation depends, they believe, on:

- their own performance;
- their previous career experience;
- organisational politics;
- luck – being there when opportunities arise;
- formal qualifications;
- corporate career planning.

These are listed in decreasing order of importance. So they think they have to work well in order to be able to seize the chance of getting out of the frying pan into what they don't perceive to be the fire.

The implications for psychological contracting of these findings are immense. Clearly, individuals feel that all or most of the four balances are tilted in the organisation's direction. Major upheavals in their organisations finally tilt the balance too far, and they change jobs or leave. Such upheavals may be associated with strategic shifts, especially those across from defender club to analyser academy, or down into reactor fortress. Certainly Nicholson and West's managers disliked most those organisations which were crisis orientated.

In these circumstances, repeated negotiation of the career contract seems crucial. Whether or not a person moves job within the organisation or outside seems largely a matter of chance at present. Those at the boundary (sales, for example), are somewhat more likely to change job, probably because more outside opportunities present themselves.[4] There may be no other jobs available in the organisation where the balance is notably different; in this case the individual will try to up sticks and away. On the other hand, organisations may seek to correct imbalances and thereby retain valued staff:

- A large insurance company, moving from defender club to analyser academy, is intent on rebalancing its intelligence–trust axis. It is very keen for its different businesses and the line managers within them to take more responsibility for their decisions. However, realising the structural and cultural change that this rebalance implies, it is willing for more resources to be spent on training and development support.

- A small group of consultants is a clear candidate for the prospector baseball team label. The main concern of this small business is with the knowledge–tolerance and intelligence–trust balances. The consultants expect each other to keep up to date with their professional knowledge and also to bring back from their assignments news of current market demands. Yet there seems to be little room for taking time out from the work schedule to keep up to date; and all the news they bring back is second-guessed by the owner of the business. The balances have tilted the organisation's way. Opportunities, however, may be there to tip other balances towards individuals: a marketer and a researcher may be brought in to *support* the consultants in the field; and the *loyalty* of the consultants in sticking with the consultancy because it's small and personal may be recognised by a profit-sharing scheme and greater choice of assignment.

A Swift fable

So the individual's task is a tricky one. Just like the organisation, the individual has his or her set of balances to keep. There are no easy answers for organisations – no quick technological fixes. Nor are quick individual fixes available. Perhaps the image to sum it all up is Gulliver on a tightrope.

Gulliver has set off on his tightrope journey – he can't remain still or he'll fall off. He can't go back because where he came from is totally destroyed by earthquake. He does have to pause for a brief second occasionally as a result of the two or three quick steps he's just taken. All the time he's trying to adjust his balance to keep himself steady. Sometimes he tries to move his head, or his arms, or his legs. Swarming all over Gulliver are the inhabitants of Lilliput, who need to cross to the other side of the chasm too, or be swallowed up by the earthquake. Gulliver can't adjust his balance himself. For the weight of the innumerable Lilliputians is such that it is *their* movements which determine whether he keeps his balance or not. When they feel a chill blast coming from the east, many of them rush across Gulliver's broad back to perch upon his east-facing shoulder. They have to dip their right shoulders into the icy wind too; but they've helped him keep his balance in the face of this threat. Other Lilliputians run on ahead of Gulliver, clearing the ice off what to them is a wide bridge but to him a thin rope. Many others form the ballast; they stay roughly between his shoulders, moving only slightly to keep their own balance too. Periodically, some Lilliputians fall off – the big step that Gulliver has just taken has been too much for them, and they have lost their tenuous hold on his body. Others find themselves isolated. They remained on Gulliver's west-facing shoulder while the others changed shoulders. They didn't fancy dipping their own right shoulders into the wind on Gulliver's other side. And anyway, some of them thought they could discern a strong westerly gale approaching in the longer term. These latter Lilliputians felt that they weren't too popular with their compatriots who'd switched shoulders. They also noted that the Lilliputians who were far ahead clearing the ice off the rope were managing to keep their balance all right. Indeed, they seemed to be enjoying themselves. Looking behind, they saw looming through the swirling mists figures which looked like Gulliver's relatives. How naive they were, they thought, to believe that he had sprung fully grown from the ocean. He must have had parents too. On looking more closely, they could discern no expressions of parental affection in these pursuers. On the contrary, some of them looked quite fierce. Several were making a very good fist of their tightrope journey. One or two, in particular, seemed to have it taped. They used a bar to balance with, and all the Lilliputians who had hitched a lift on them were riding upon it. These Lilliputians all held hands in a long line, and moved one step to the right or to the left as the balance required. Now, thought our heroes, what shall we do? Shall we stick with Gulliver and continue to warn of the west wind approaching? Shall we volunteer to go and clear the ice off the rope for him? Shall we slip quietly down his leg and walk on our own behind him, with a couple of mates? Or shall we wait and hitch a lift from one of his relatives whose Lilliputians have collaborated to keep the balance? They each made their choice – but the wise ones knew that the other side of the chasm didn't exist. There was no end to the journey.

Some final questions and suggestions

- Read back over the questions you answered at the end of each of the previous chapters, and reflect on the answers you gave. Do you feel that you are at a point in your organisational career where you need to renegotiate your psychological contract with your employer?
- Are you clear about the current state of each of the four balances in your organisation? In your particular part of it? Are they likely to remain roughly the same in the short and medium term or to change as a result of a strategic shift? If change, in which direction?
- Are you clear about your own priorities with respect to the balances? Do they accord with your career anchor and your current non-work roles? Are there any likely changes in your life which will alter these priorities?
- How well do your own priorities and those of the organisation fit? Does the degree of misfit imply no change? A role change? A job change? A change of employer?
- How likely are you to succeed in negotiating these changes in the light of the labour market situation in your occupation; in your sector; in your organisation? Are you in a seller's or a buyer's market?
- What strategy and tactics are you going to use in the negotiations?

Notes

1 G. Golzen and A. Garner (1990) *Smart Moves*. Oxford: Basil Blackwell. (Quotes from pp. 3 and 6).

2 P. Herriot (1989) *Recruitment in the 90s*. London: IPM Press.

3 N. Nicholson and M. West (1989) *Managerial Job Change: Men and Women in Transition*. Cambridge: Cambridge University Press.

4 M. Granovetter (1980) 'Labor mobility, internal markets, and job matching: a comparison of the sociological and economic approaches', *Research in Social Stratification and Mobility*, 5: 3–39. Greenwich, Connecticut: JAI Press.

Author Index

Subject Index